CHRONICLES OF THE FORCE

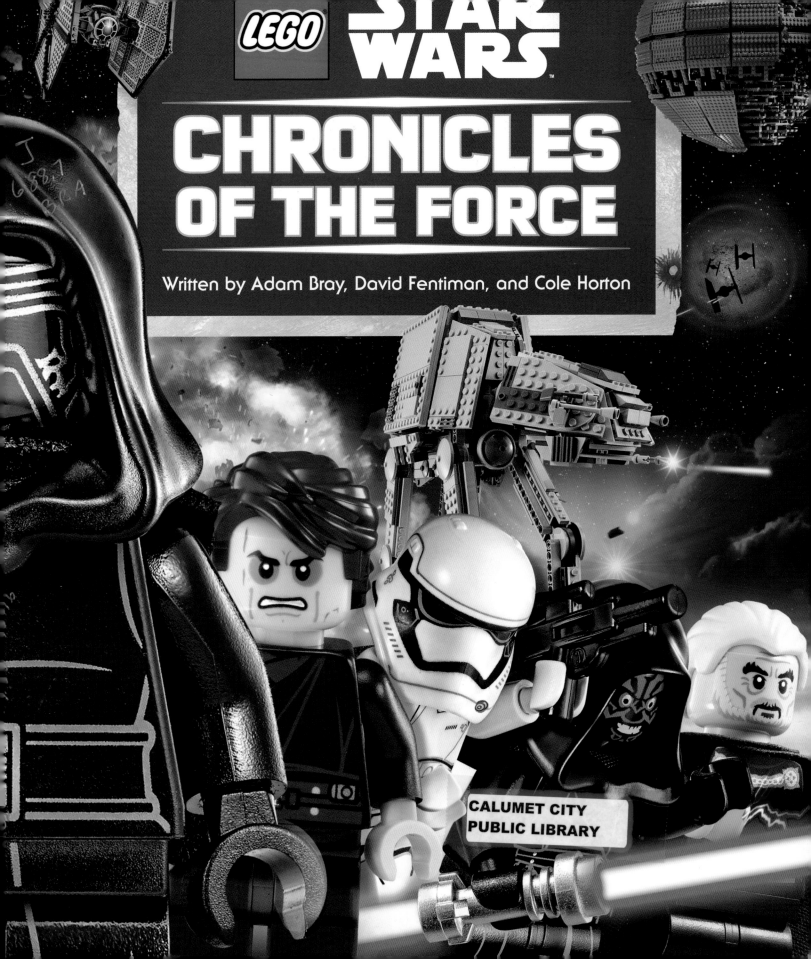

LEGO® STAR WARS™

CHRONICLES OF THE FORCE

Written by Adam Bray, David Fentiman, and Cole Horton

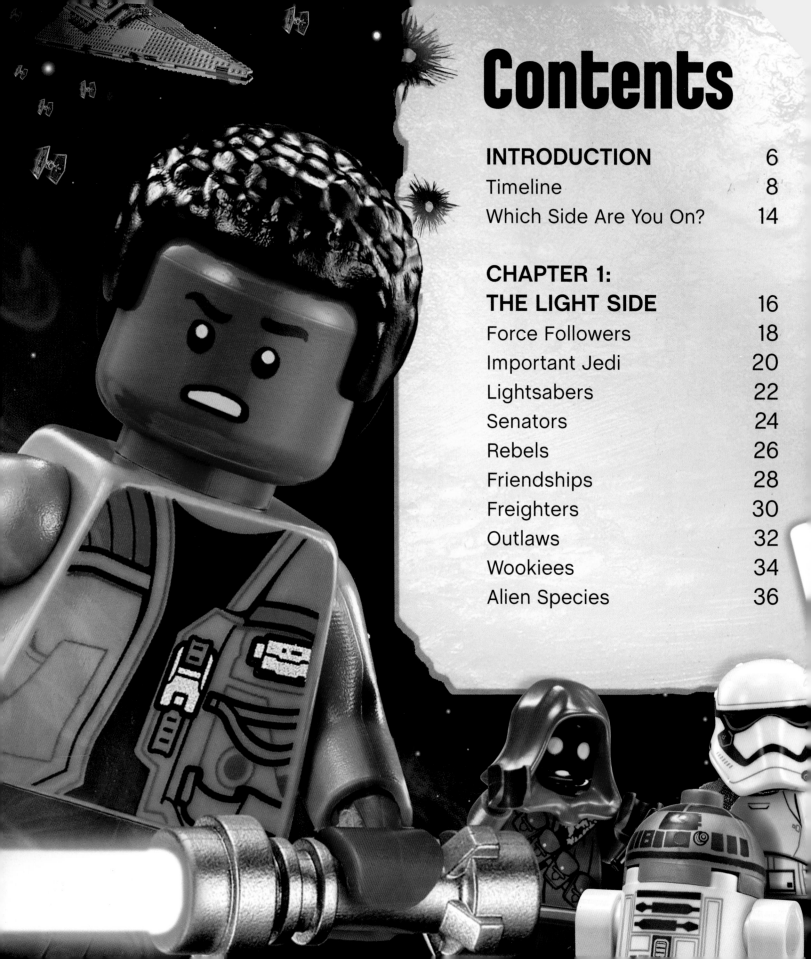

Contents

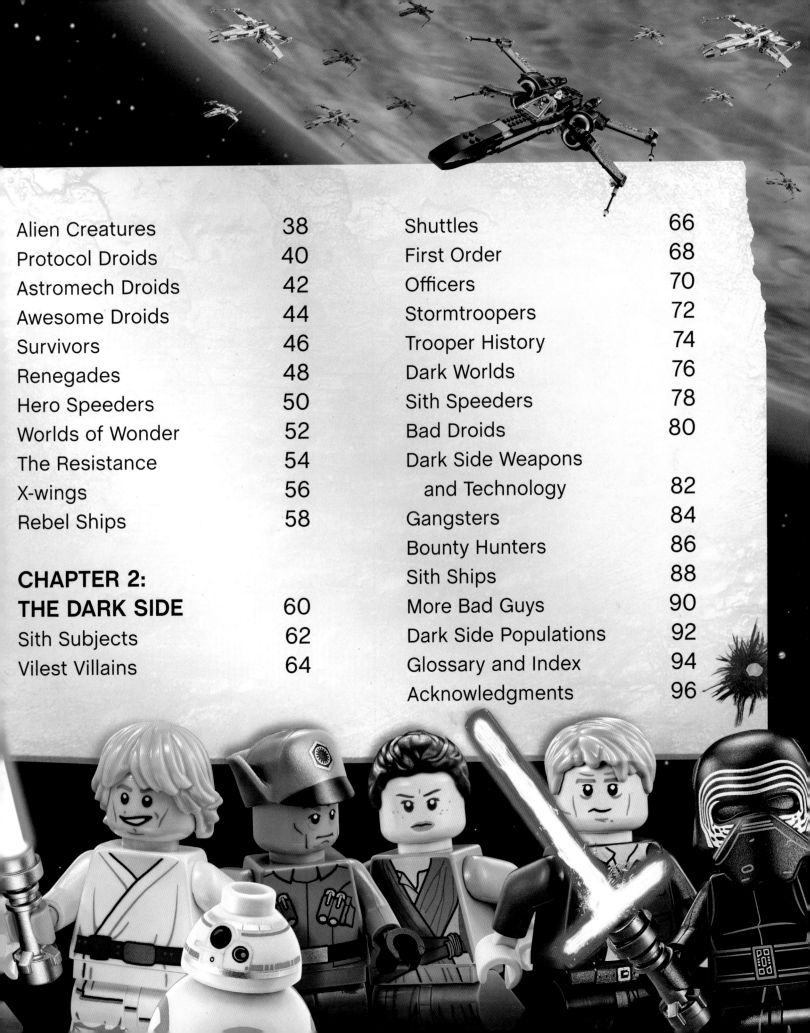

UNKAR'S BRUTE

INTRODUCTION

A galaxy in turmoil. Again.

The First Order is terrifying the people of the galaxy. Stormtrooper armies are massing for battle. Their mysterious leaders lurk in the shadows.

Many heroes of old have been called back into action. What secrets from the past can they teach us? What lost wisdom is there to discover? Which events have shaped the galaxy over the course of history? Will the light side triumph once more?

It is time to find out.

Delve into the entire LEGO® *Star Wars*™ story in the *Chronicles of the Force*.

TIMELINE

THE GALAXY IS full of heroes, villains, tragic tales, and triumphs. One family has seen more than their share of amazing events. From the old days of the Republic to the struggle against the First Order, the journey of the Skywalkers, their friends, and their foes is an epic saga.

CRISIS IN THE REPUBLIC
Spans Episodes I and II

THE CLONE WARS
Spans Episode II, *The Clone Wars*, and Episode III

THE REBELS ERA
Spans *Star Wars Rebels*

THE EMPIRE ERA
Spans Episode III and Episodes IV to VI

THE NEW REPUBLIC ERA
Begins with Episode VII

THE REPUBLIC
For over a thousand generations, the Jedi have served as guardians of peace and justice in the Republic. They use the power of the Force, a mystical energy field that binds the universe together, to fight the evil Sith.

BATTLE OF GEONOSIS
Anakin and Padmé take on the Trade Federation and the Separatists at the Battle of Geonosis. The Jedi fight the Separatists' droid army with an army of clones, beginning the Clone Wars.

BATTLE FOR NABOO
When the evil Trade Federation blockades Naboo, Queen Padmé Amidala saves her people, aided by the Jedi and a young Anakin Skywalker. Anakin leaves his home on Tatooine to learn about the ways of the Force from the Jedi.

LEAVE MY PEOPLE ALONE!

PADMÉ AMIDALA

A GALAXY DIVIDED
Count Dooku rallies the people of the galaxy to leave the Republic and form the Confederacy of Independent Systems. This Separatist split is actually devised by the Republic's leader, Chancellor Palpatine, who is secretly the Sith Lord Darth Sidious.

YODA

JEDI GENERALS

With the Clone Wars raging, the peaceful Jedi must go to battle. Anakin, Yoda, Obi-Wan Kenobi, and other Jedi struggle against the Separatists, the Sith, and battle droids to restore peace to the Republic.

DON'T MESS WITH THE LIGHT SIDE.

OBI-WAN KENOBI

ANAKIN AND AHSOKA

When the Jedi Council gives Anakin his own Padawan apprentice, he doesn't know what to do! But Anakin and Ahsoka make a great team and are known for their heroics during the Clone Wars.

FALLEN JEDI

Anakin has turned to the dark side. He loses in a lightsaber duel with Obi-Wan on the planet Mustafar. Badly injured, Anakin is encased in a suit of armor, becoming Darth Vader. His wife Padmé secretly gives birth to twins, Luke and Leia.

CLONES

The loyal clones are the unsung heroes of the Clone Wars. On worlds and starships across the galaxy, they fight for the Republic under the command of brave Jedi generals.

ORDER 66

Darth Sidious has secretly programmed the clones to turn on their Jedi masters at his command. He issues Order 66 and thousands of Jedi are defeated in fierce battles against their once-loyal clone troopers.

SECRET SITH REVEALED

The Jedi hunt the secret leader of the Separatists for years, not realizing that it was Chancellor Palpatine all along. When Anakin finds out, it is too late! Mace Windu and the rest of the Jedi Council are not powerful enough to defeat the Sith Lord.

CHANCELLOR PALPATINE

ALL OF THE GALAXY WILL BE MINE!

REBELS UNITE

Brave rebels Hera, Kanan, Zeb, Sabine, and their astromech droid Chopper, meet young Ezra Bridger on the planet Lothal. When Kanan realizes that Ezra is strong in the Force, he takes him on as his apprentice.

FURRY FRIENDS

The rebels fight hard to combat the evil Empire. When they save a band of Wookiees from slavery on the planet Kessel, Kanan's Jedi powers are exposed to the Empire.

UNWANTED ATTENTION

The Imperials send an evil Inquisitor to hunt down Kanan, as well as his rebel friends. The Inquisitor is trained in the Force and skilled with a lightsaber. But ultimately, he is no match for Kanan, who defeats him.

THE REBEL'S FIRST VICTORY

A Rebel Alliance is formed and soon steals the plans to the Empire's battle station, the Death Star. Now an adult, Leia has joined the rebels. She is caught by Darth Vader as she tries to deliver the plans to Obi-Wan Kenobi. She manages to hide the plans in astromech droid R2-D2.

RISE OF THE EMPIRE

With the Jedi all but destroyed and the galaxy in chaos, Chancellor Palpatine declares himself Emperor. With Darth Vader at his side, the secret Sith seeks to expand his empire and hunt down the last of the Jedi.

NOT ANOTHER DREADFUL ADVENTURE!

C-3PO

CURSE YOU, REBELS!

DARTH VADER

THE BATTLE OF YAVIN
Piloting an X-wing starfighter, Luke Skywalker and the rebels mount a daring attack on the Death Star. Han Solo and Chewbacca show up to help save the day, freeing Luke to blow up the giant battle station.

VADER DEFEATS OBI-WAN
Obi-Wan and Darth Vader duel on the Death Star. Obi-Wan sacrifices himself to allow Luke, Leia, Han, and the droids to escape. They deliver the stolen plans to the Rebel Alliance and discover that the Death Star has a weakness!

BEEP-BOOP BLOOP!

R2-D2

AN UNLIKELY ALLY
Luke and Obi-Wan hire Han Solo to take them to the Rebel Alliance. Han is the captain of the *Millennium Falcon*, one of the fastest starships in the galaxy. Along with his Wookiee copilot Chewbacca, they find the Death Star and rescue Princess Leia.

A NEW HOPE
R2-D2 and his fellow droid C-3PO escape when their ship is raided by Imperial forces. They land on Tatooine where they meet Luke Skywalker. Together, they deliver the stolen Death Star plans to Master Kenobi, who is in hiding on the planet. Obi-Wan urges Luke to join him and learn about the ways of the Force.

LUKE SKYWALKER

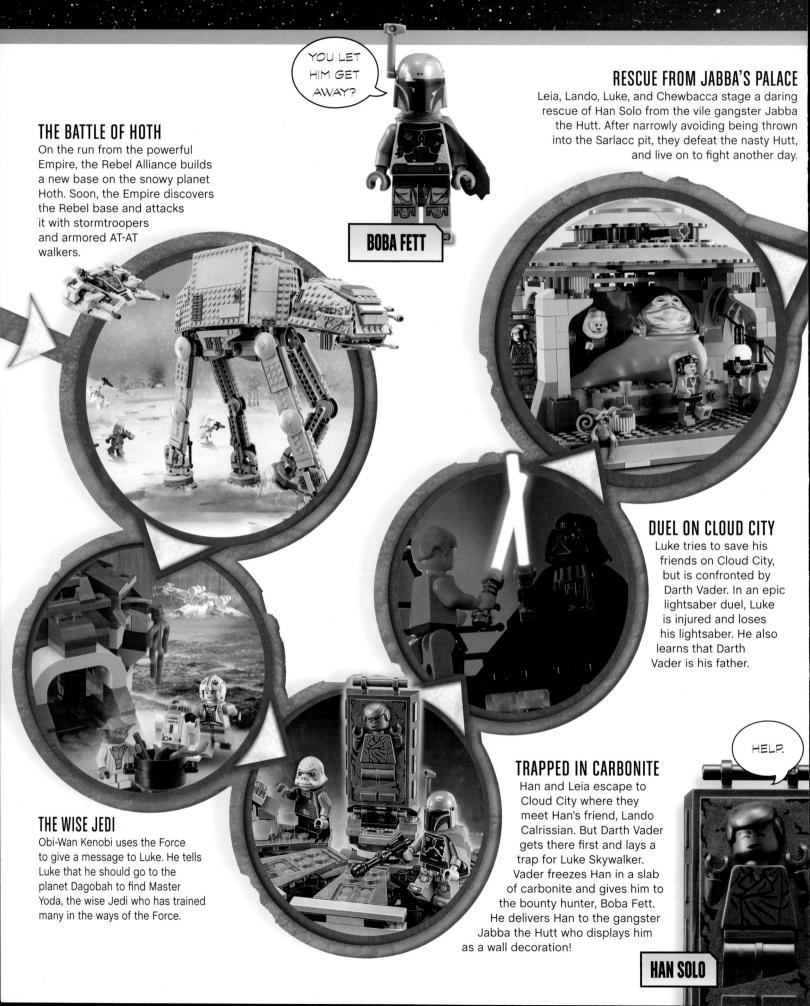

THE BATTLE OF HOTH

On the run from the powerful Empire, the Rebel Alliance builds a new base on the snowy planet Hoth. Soon, the Empire discovers the Rebel base and attacks it with stormtroopers and armored AT-AT walkers.

YOU LET HIM GET AWAY?

BOBA FETT

RESCUE FROM JABBA'S PALACE

Leia, Lando, Luke, and Chewbacca stage a daring rescue of Han Solo from the vile gangster Jabba the Hutt. After narrowly avoiding being thrown into the Sarlacc pit, they defeat the nasty Hutt, and live on to fight another day.

DUEL ON CLOUD CITY

Luke tries to save his friends on Cloud City, but is confronted by Darth Vader. In an epic lightsaber duel, Luke is injured and loses his lightsaber. He also learns that Darth Vader is his father.

THE WISE JEDI

Obi-Wan Kenobi uses the Force to give a message to Luke. He tells Luke that he should go to the planet Dagobah to find Master Yoda, the wise Jedi who has trained many in the ways of the Force.

TRAPPED IN CARBONITE

Han and Leia escape to Cloud City where they meet Han's friend, Lando Calrissian. But Darth Vader gets there first and lays a trap for Luke Skywalker. Vader freezes Han in a slab of carbonite and gives him to the bounty hunter, Boba Fett. He delivers Han to the gangster Jabba the Hutt who displays him as a wall decoration!

HELP.

HAN SOLO

ATTACK ON ENDOR

The Rebel Alliance discovers that the Emperor is building a second Death Star over the forest moon of Endor. They must destroy the battle station—and the Emperor aboard it—to bring peace and justice to the galaxy once more. In a daring raid, Leia, Han, and Luke shut down the energy shield that protects the Death Star, while Lando Calrissian leads the attack in space, destroying the battle station.

THE FORCE AWAKENS

A Jakku scavenger named Rey and a First Order deserter named Finn meet on Jakku. They embark on a galactic adventure that sees them face the might of the First Order.

BB-8

THERE IS ANOTHER

Before leaving to face Darth Vader, Luke reveals some shocking news to Leia: They are actually brother and sister. The Force is indeed strong in their family! Luke must leave Leia and the rebels on Endor to confront Vader and the Emperor once and for all.

RISE OF THE RESISTANCE

Princess Leia has created a group known as the Resistance to guard against the First Order. She sends her best pilot, Poe Dameron, with his astromech droid BB-8, on a secret mission to the planet Jakku.

ANAKIN REDEEMED

Darth Vader and Luke duel once again. Luke refuses to give in to the dark side, so the Emperor attempts to destroy him with Force lightning. Vader sees his son's pain and turns on the Sith Lord, throwing the Emperor down a reactor shaft to his doom. Although he doesn't survive the ordeal, Vader is redeemed by his heroic deed.

A NEW BATTLE

Thirty years after the Battle of Endor, the galaxy is at peace. But the remnants of the Empire have formed a new army known as the First Order, and they are plotting their revenge.

WHICH SIDE

THE GALAXY IS full of heroes, villains, and everything in between. Will you choose the light side of the Force and follow the path of the Jedi? Will you take the quick and easy path to unlimited power by following the dark side of the Force? Or will you make your own path as a pirate or bounty hunter? Make your choices to find out!

ARE YOU READY FOR AN ADVENTURE?

YES

NO

ARE YOU MOTIVATED BY MONEY, GREED, OR POWER?

NO

YES

ARE YOU GOOD AT TAKING ORDERS?

NO

LIGHT SIDE

You are the guardian of peace and justice. Like Poe, you fight for the light side to make the galaxy a better place!

MOISTURE FARMER

You don't need a foolish, idealistic crusade. It's better staying home on a moisture farm like Uncle Owen.

ARE YOU ON?

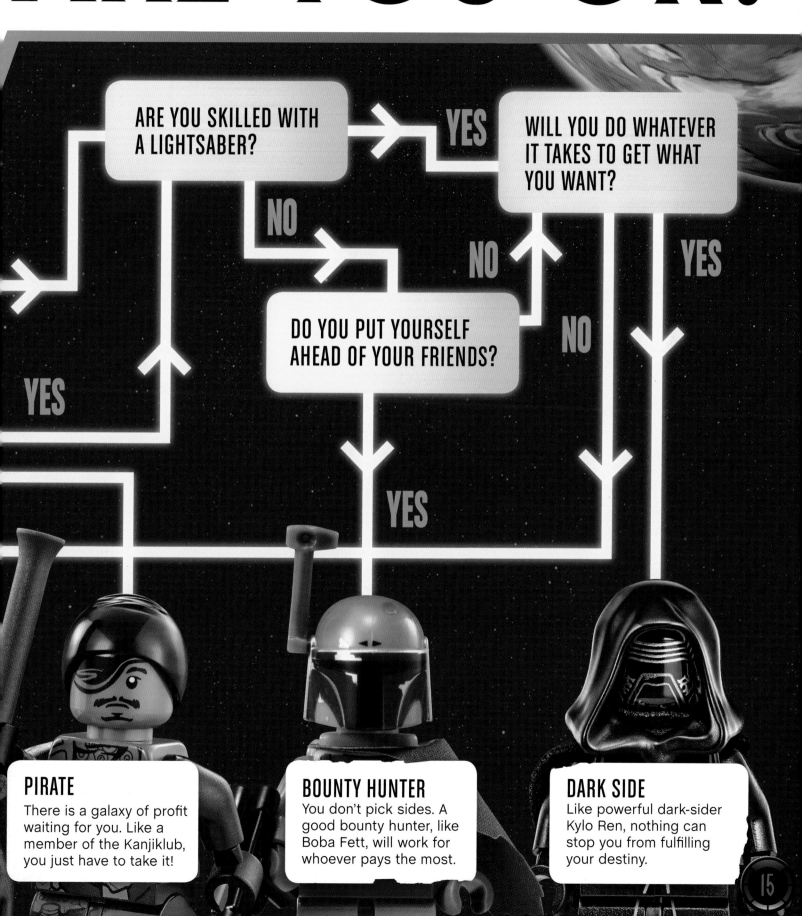

ARE YOU SKILLED WITH A LIGHTSABER?

YES

WILL YOU DO WHATEVER IT TAKES TO GET WHAT YOU WANT?

NO

NO

YES

DO YOU PUT YOURSELF AHEAD OF YOUR FRIENDS?

NO

YES

YES

YES

PIRATE
There is a galaxy of profit waiting for you. Like a member of the Kanjiklub, you just have to take it!

BOUNTY HUNTER
You don't pick sides. A good bounty hunter, like Boba Fett, will work for whoever pays the most.

DARK SIDE
Like powerful dark-sider Kylo Ren, nothing can stop you from fulfilling your destiny.

THE LIGHT SIDE

TOP 4
Force power rankings

1 ### ANAKIN SKYWALKER
Believed to be the "Chosen One," Anakin has incredible Force potential, even as a child.

2 ### YODA
Though small in stature, Yoda is one of the most powerful Force users in the entire galaxy.

3 ### DARTH SIDIOUS
This scheming dark side wielder proves himself a match for Yoda when they have an epic Force duel.

4 ### LUKE SKYWALKER
A gifted Force user, Luke's ability is in his genes—but his Force strength has never been fully measured.

FORCE

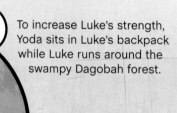

YODA'S FORCE TRAINING REGIME
How to train a Jedi

1 To increase Luke's strength, Yoda sits in Luke's backpack while Luke runs around the swampy Dagobah forest.

2 Yoda's training technique for teaching Luke concentration skills? Making Luke perform a handstand, while he perches on his feet!

3 Yoda uses the Force to lift Luke's enormous X-wing starfighter out of a swamp. This shows Luke the immense power of the Force.

FORCE KNOWLEDGE

FORCE ESCAPE
When Luke finds himself dangling from the roof of a hungry wampa's cave, he uses his Force powers to retrieve his lightsaber from the icy cave floor. The Hoth Wampa Cave (set 8089) has a built-in firing mechanism for the lightsaber to shoot out from!

STRANGE

After death, some people who are strong in the Force can become a Force ghost. When Obi-Wan appears as one, he tells Luke to find Yoda on the planet Dagobah.

FOLLOWERS

FROM NOBLE JEDI to sinister Sith, the Force is strong with these galactic warriors who use their powers to change the galaxy, for better or for worse.

FORCE FACTS

Name: Luke Skywalker

Affiliation: Jedi Knight, Rebel Alliance

Mentors: Obi-Wan Kenobi, Yoda

Loyal sidekick: R2-D2

Relatives: It's complicated

REALLY?!
Luke lost his original blue lightsaber in a duel with Darth Vader. He later replaced it with a green one.

AWESOME!
Force potential is measured in midi-chlorians—microscopic life forms that live inside the cells of all living things.

THE UNIVERSE IN UNITS
20,000
Anakin's midi-chlorian count, making him strong with the Force

JEDI TEACHER
After the Battle of Endor, Luke begins a school to train a new generation of Jedi. Unfortunately, everything he has built is eventually destroyed by Kylo Ren, and Luke vanishes.

IMPORTANT JEDI

USING FANTASTIC FORCE powers and noble knowledge, the brave Jedi are the guardians of peace and justice in the galaxy.

FORCE KNOWLEDGE

For thousands of years, Jedi were trained in awesome Jedi temples. While hiding on Dagobah, Yoda must teach Luke Skywalker the ways of the Force in his humble hut home.

JEDI FAMILY

Jedi are wise, well trained, and never boring. These alien Jedi come from all corners of the galaxy!

Ahsoka Tano, Togruta Padawan of Anakin Skywalker.

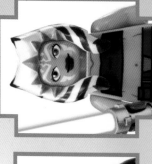

Aayla Secura, Twi'lek Jedi Master during the Clone Wars.

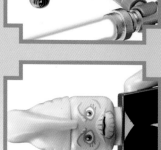

Jedi Master Rusty is an Ithorian, a species that has T-shaped heads.

Ki-Adi-Mundi, a Cerean Jedi Master with the biggest head on the Jedi Council.

WHO TRAINED WHOM?

Yoda trains hundreds of Jedi, including Count Dooku. As a Jedi, Dooku takes Qui-Gon Jinn as his Padawan. Dooku later falls to the dark side. Once a Knight, Qui-Gon takes Obi-Wan as his apprentice. Qui-Gon is defeated in battle on Naboo. Obi-Wan promises Qui-Gon that he will train Anakin.

YODA

STRANGE

Ki-Adi-Mundi has two hearts to pump blood to his very large and very complex brain.

COUNT DOOKU

FORCE KNOWLEDGE

SECRET GUARDIAN

After the fall of the Republic and the destruction of the Jedi Order, Obi-Wan changes his name to "Ben" and hides on Tatooine. There, he watches over young Luke Skywalker from a distance.

FORCE FACTS

Name: Obi-Wan Kenobi

Affiliation: Jedi Knight

Mentors: Qui-Gon Jinn and Yoda

Main enemy: General Grievous

Favorite hiding spot: Tatooine

"ADVENTURE. EXCITEMENT.
A JEDI
CRAVES NOT THESE THINGS."

YODA

BRICK-SIZED FACT

Anakin's Jedi Interceptor is the first Jedi interceptor with a slot for a full-size astromech droid and flick-fire missiles.

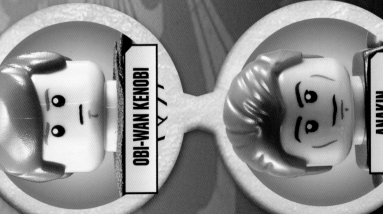

QUI-GON JINN

OBI-WAN KENOBI

ANAKIN SKYWALKER

TOP 6
Awesome lightsabers

1 THE ELECTRIFYING ONE
Kylo Ren's lightsaber is like no other—it has three fiery blades.

2 THE DOUBLE TROUBLE ONE
One blade just isn't enough for scary Sith Darth Maul.

3 THE FANCY ONE
Count Dooku's red lightsaber has an elegant curved handle.

4 THE MYSTERIOUS ONE
The ancient Darksaber has a black energy blade.

5 THE UNIQUE ONE
Mace Windu wields a rare purple lightsaber, different from his fellow Jedi.

6 THE CURVY ONES
The deadly assassin Asajj Ventress has curvy hilts on her two lightsabers.

FORCE FACTS
Name: Mace Windu
Affiliation: Jedi
Species: Human
Homeworld: Haruun Kal
Abilities: Lightsaber combat, talking things through

FORCE KNOWLEDGE

CRYSTAL POWER
Lightsabers are powered by crystals. The blades glow either blue, like Ahsoka Tano's, green, like Qui-Gon Jinn's, or rarely, another color, like Mace Windu's purple blade.

BRICK-SIZED FACT
Some lightsabers are equipped with a bulb that lights up the "blade" when the minifigure's head is clicked.

MACE WINDU'S FORCE SKILL — LIGHTSABERS — WISDOM — SPOTTING SITH LORDS

SABERS

WHAT'S THE BEST thing about using the Force? Wielding a lightsaber! This ancient energy weapon is used by Jedi, Sith, and other Force users in combat.

LIGHTSABER VERSUS LIGHTNING

Legendary Jedi Master Mace Windu is known throughout the galaxy for his amazing skill with a lightsaber. But not even his unique purple blade can withstand the dark side power of evil Sith Lord Darth Sidious.

FORCE FACTS

Name: Darth Maul

Affiliation: Sith

Master: Darth Sidious

Homeworld: Dathomir

Main enemy: Obi-Wan Kenobi

> " **THIS WEAPON** IS YOUR LIFE. "
>
> OBI-WAN KENOBI TO ANAKIN SKYWALKER

Q & A

What weapons can defeat a lightsaber?

MagnaGuards (General Grievous' terrifying bodyguards) wield a powerful electrostaff. It has deadly energy flowing through it that can deflect lightsabers.

THE UNIVERSE IN UNITS

2

The number of minifigures that wield a Darksaber: Darth Maul and Pre Vizsla. The Darksaber is a mysterious weapon that was stolen from the Jedi long ago.

NO WAY!

Darth Maul's double-bladed lightsaber still works after it has been chopped in half!

Q & A

Which politician leads the Rebellion?

Mon Mothma is the leader of the Alliance and later serves as Chancellor of the New Republic.

> **"I'D BE MUCH TOO FRIGHTENED TO TEASE A SENATOR."**
>
> ANAKIN SKYWALKER

FORCE FACTS

Name: Leia Organa

Affiliation: Rebel Alliance/Resistance

Profession: Politician, secret rebel leader, Resistance general

Skills: Inspiring others, shooting a blaster, arguing with Han Solo

THE UNIVERSE IN UNITS

11

Ion turbine engines on the *Tantive IV*, a favorite ship of politicians like Princess Leia

FROM PRINCESS TO GENERAL

After the defeat of the Empire, Leia becomes a senator in the New Republic. During the rise of the First Order, however, Leia leaves the Senate to become the leader of the Resistance.

SENATORS

LOOKING FOR A LEADER? Wise politicians like Senator Leia Organa help keep law and order throughout the galaxy, inspiring their people even during dark times.

You might be a SENATOR if...

1. YOU TRY TO PUT EVERYTHING TO A VOTE
2. YOU ALWAYS WANT TO GIVE A SPEECH
3. YOU'D MUCH RATHER HAVE A DEBATE THAN A LIGHTSABER DUEL

OOPS!

Senator Jar Jar Binks accidently voted to give Chancellor Palpatine the power to take over the Republic.

CORUSCANT
The planet Coruscant is the home of the Senate. Senators from all over the galaxy gather here to discuss important issues.

TOP 4
Leia hairstyles

1. BUNS
Leia's classic look. Two braids, each coiled into a bun.

2. HIGH BRAID
A no-nonsense style for a busy senator.

3. STRAIGHT
Leia lets her hair down when hanging out with Ewoks.

4. FRENCH BRAID
Leia is ready for battle in this sensible style.

THE EVOLUTION OF... DARTH SIDIOUS

FAMILY TIES
Leia's mother, Padmé Amidala, served in the Republic Senate for many years. Leia unknowingly follows in her mother's footsteps when she chooses to become a senator.

CHANCELLOR
Palpatine is elected leader of the Republic.

CAPTIVE
The Chancellor is captured by the Separatists during the Clone Wars.

SECRET SITH
The Jedi discover Palpatine is not just a politician.

EMPEROR
He declares himself Emperor of the galaxy.

REBELS

THE EMPIRE IMPOSES strict rules and harsh punishments throughout the galaxy—and some people decide enough is enough! Small groups begin to speak out and fight back, eventually forming the Rebel Alliance...

REALLY?!

The war between the Empire and the Rebel Alliance doesn't end after the Battle of Endor. The fight continues until a major battle above Jakku.

BEFORE THE START OF **THE REBEL ALLIANCE**

AHSOKA TANO
The Jedi trains a rebel group on the planet Onderon during the Clone Wars.

PADMÉ AMIDALA
Padmé and a small group of fellow senators try to disrupt Palpatine's evil Clone Wars plans.

HERA SYNDULLA
Twi'lek Hera forms a small rebel unit to challenge the might of the Empire.

KANAN JARRUS
Kanan and his new rebel team destroy Moff Tarkin's Imperial ship.

LEIA ORGANA
The teenage princess assists her adoptive father, Bail Organa, on secret rebel missions.

REBEL SOLDIER TYPES

OFFICERS
Lead the troops at rebel bases and out onto the battlefield.

SCOUT TROOPERS
Serve in the field or aboard starships like *Tantive IV*.

HOTH TROOPERS
Ready for battle against Imperial snowtroopers on icy planets.

ENDOR TROOPERS
Ready for battle in forests and other wooded environments.

FORCE FACTS

Name: Gial Ackbar

Occupation: Admiral

Affiliation: Rebel Alliance/Resistance

Species: Mon Calamari

Homeworld: Mon Cala

Abilities: Military strategy, leadership

TOP 5
Rebel heroes

1. MON MOTHMA
Supreme Commander of the Rebel Alliance.

2. ADMIRAL ACKBAR
Leads the assault on the second Death Star from the rebel flagship.

3. GENERAL CRIX MADINE
He is the rebel general who selects Han Solo to lead the important rebel mission on Endor.

4. GENERAL RIEEKAN
Founding member of the Rebel Alliance and commanding officer at Echo Base.

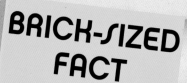

5. PRINCESS LEIA
Senator who transports the Death Star plans to the rebel leaders.

BRICK-SIZED FACT
In sets, Admiral Ackbar always appears with a LEGO® coffee cup.

NO WAY!
Some rebels started out as Imperial officers. Biggs Darklighter, Thane Kyrell, and General Madine all defected from the Empire!

> " YOU'RE A PART OF THE **REBEL ALLIANCE,** AND A **TRAITOR.** "
>
> DARTH VADER TO PRINCESS LEIA

PALACE RESCUE

Is that bounty hunter Boushh coming to Han's rescue at Jabba's palace? No, it's Princess Leia in disguise! She poses as an ally of Jabba the Hutt to rescue Han from the gangster.

SARLACC SAVIOR

Lando Calrissian was once a smuggler before he joined the Rebel Alliance. Disguised as one of Jabba the Hutt's guards, Lando rescues Luke Skywalker from the jaws of the Sarlacc beast.

BETRAYAL

As the Baron Administrator of Cloud City, Lando Calrissian is sometimes a dangerous friend to have. On the planet Bespin, Lando betrays his friend Han, who ends up frozen in carbonite.

FRIENDSHIPS

THERE ARE DANGERS lurking in every corner of the galaxy. With so much unrest, it's important to have good friends to look out for you, and help save the day when things get tough.

WHO'S WHO IN THE SKYWALKER FAMILY

The fate of the galaxy is linked to the Skywalker family. Their romantic partnerships have helped to change the course of history.

ANAKIN SKYWALKER

PADMÉ AMIDALA

LUKE SKYWALKER

LEIA ORGANA

HAN SOLO

FORCE FACTS

Name: *Han Solo*

Affiliation: *Rebel Alliance/Resistance*

Species: *Human*

Homeworld: *Corellia*

Abilities: *Pilot, marksman, entrepreneur*

REALLY?!

When Han Solo rescues Chewbacca from the Empire, Chewie promises to look out for Han for the rest of his life.

THE EVOLUTION OF... HAN SOLO

YOUNG HAN

Legends say that, as a child, Han escapes from an orphanage and leads a group of young Jedi on a misadventure.

ROGUE HAN

Now smugglers, Han Solo and his pal Chewie get caught up in a quest to save a princess.

OLDER HAN

Han is old and gray, but still flying the *Millennium Falcon*—now with Rey and Finn aboard.

FREIGHTERS

EVERY GOOD PILOT needs a great ship. From small cruisers to the big Corellian ships, these freighters move cargo, people, and droids throughout the galaxy.

MILLENNIUM FALCON

The *Millennium Falcon* sometimes malfunctions, but its owner Han Solo doesn't mind. When Rey and Finn find the *Falcon* and use it to escape from Jakku, they are caught in a tractor beam from Han's own cargo ship!

"**GET ABOARD AND PRIME THE ENGINES...** ASSUMING IT *HAS* ENGINES."

ANAKIN SKYWALKER TO HIS PADAWAN AHSOKA TANO ABOUT THE *TWILIGHT*

BRICK-SIZED FACT
The Ultimate Collector's Series *Millennium Falcon* is built entirely to the scale of minifigures and is the second largest LEGO set ever made, with 5,195 pieces.

AWESOME!
Han Solo won the *Millennium Falcon* from his old friend Lando Calrissian in the card game sabacc!

311

Pages of instructions for building the Ultimate Collector's Series *Millennium Falcon* set

REALLY?!

Freighter pilots pass the time by playing games like holochess. But it's no fun playing against a Wookiee—they have been known to become extremely angry when they lose!

NEW OWNERS

Han Solo lost the *Millennium Falcon* after the Rebellion was over. It ended up in the hands of the vicious Jakku junk dealer Unkar Plutt.

FAMOUS REBEL CORELLIAN FREIGHTERS

THE *GHOST* ▲

Owned by the rebel Hera Syndulla and home base to her loyal crew, the *Ghost* has two huge rocket boosters and an escape pod in case of emergencies.

TANTIVE IV ▼

Senator Bail Organa is the proud owner of this ship, with Captain Antilles as pilot. Unfortunately for the rebels, it is later captured by Darth Vader!

THE *TWILIGHT* ▲

Anakin Skywalker found the *Twilight* on a landing platform on the planet Teth. He gave it much needed upgrades, including three blaster cannons and a tow hook for hauling large cargo.

OUTLAWS

SMUGGLERS, CRIMINALS, LIARS, and cheats—the galaxy is full of not-so-good guys. And many of them can be found on the planet Tatooine. Some hide in the shadows, while others jump out when you least expect it. Wherever they are, keep away... if you can!

TOP 3

Boonta Eve podrace finish times

1 ANAKIN SKYWALKER
15 minutes, 44 seconds

2 GASGANO
15 minutes, 49 seconds

3 ALDAR BEEDO
15 minutes, 52 seconds

NOTE: Sebulba's podracer is destroyed and he does not finish the race!

CANTINA CROWD

Tatooine's Mos Eisley Cantina is famous as a hangout for outlaws. Bounty hunters and smugglers hold secret meetings here, while the Bith band plays and pickpockets lurk.

FORCE FACTS

Name: Figrin D'an

Occupation: Kloo horn player and leader of the Modal Nodes band

Affiliation: Intergalactic Federation of Musicians

Species: Bith

Homeworld: Clak'dor VII

Abilities: Bossy but effective band leader

> " **MOS EISLEY SPACEPORT...** YOU'LL NEVER FIND A MORE WRETCHED HIVE OF SCUM AND **VILLAINY.** "
>
> OBI-WAN TO LUKE

PODRACING

Podracing is a fast-paced sport, and most podracers want only one thing: to win. Especially the Boonta Eve podrace, the biggest podracing event in the galaxy. Sebulba is so desperate to win, he even sabotages his rivals' podracers!

THE UNIVERSE IN UNITS
515MPH
Maximum speed of Sebulba's podracer

NO WAY!
Podracing is illegal on most Core Worlds, partly because it's so dangerous. Many drivers can't even finish their race!

STRANGE

Some outlaws aren't all bad. Han Solo is a well-known smuggler, but he ends up joining the rebels and becoming a hero!

REALLY?!

Bounty hunter Greedo spends a lot of time in the Cantina. He knew Anakin Skywalker years ago, when the boy was a slave on Tatooine.

CANTINA IN NUMBERS ● ● ● ●

40 people
In the line to the restroom on a busy night at the Cantina

8 minifigures
Included in the Mos Eisley Cantina (set 75052)

3 instruments
For the Bith band: Kloo horn, Fizzz, and Omni box

1 droid scanner
To keep out unwanted droids

WOOKIEES

HAIRY WOOKIEES LIVE on the forest planet Kashyyyk. They are famous for their fine craftsmanship and top navigational skills. These fierce warriors are also not afraid to fight for what they believe in!

EE CHEE WA MAA!

Chewbacca makes a cameo appearance in THE LEGO® MOVIE™ alongside Han Solo, Lando Calrissian, and C-3PO.

TOP 4
Wookiee weapons

1 BOWCASTER ▶
This traditional Wookiee crossbow has a bowstring that fires energy-packed bolts.

2 KASHYYYK LONG-GUN ▼
This long-gun shoots powerful projectile blasts at short range!

3 SPEAR ▼
A simple weapon from more peaceful times. Spears are generally better for hunting than for big battles.

4 HEAVY BOWCASTER ▼
Chewbacca's automatic bowcaster breaks with Wookiee tradition as it is made with off-world technology.

FORCE FACTS

Name: Chewbacca

Species: Wookiee

Occupation: Smuggler

Affiliation: Rebel Alliance/ Resistance

Abilities: Mechanic, pilot

THE UNIVERSE IN UNITS
45,000,000
Population of Kashyyyk

" IT'S NOT WISE TO UPSET A WOOKIEE."

HAN SOLO TO C-3PO

TECH BOX

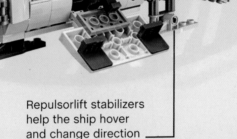

Secondary cockpit for copilot

Main pilot cockpit

Sureggi twin laser cannons

Repulsorlift stabilizers help the ship hover and change direction

WOOKIEE GUNSHIP

This Wookiee gunship is made by Appazanna Engineering Works on Kashyyyk, and decorated with traditional Wookiee clan designs. Powerful thrust engines enable the ship to fly up to 950kph (590mph)!

FORCE NUMBERS ● ● ● ●

200 years old
Chewbacca's age at the Battle of Yavin

18 sets
Include a Chewbacca minifigure

13 ammo cases
On Chewbacca's LEGO bandolier (shoulder belt)

3 legs
On the AT-AP (set 75043), a walker vehicle driven by Wookiees

FORCE KNOWLEDGE

Courageous Wookiees help the Republic fend off the Separatist invasion of their homeland—until the Republic's own clone troopers turn against them during the Battle of Kashyyyk!

WOOKIEE ROUNDUP

WOOKIEE SLAVE ▶
Some poor Wookiees are taken prisoner by the Empire to work in the toxic mines of the planet Kessel.

▲
WULFWARRO
Leader of the Wookiee slaves, Wulfwarro was rescued from slavery by former Jedi Padawan Kanan Jarrus.

◀ ### CHIEF TARFFUL
This strong Wookiee chief leads his fellow Wookiees in the Battle of Kashyyyk. He is a longtime friend of Chewbacca.

◀ ### WOOKIEE WARRIORS
This Wookiee warrior is part of a vast army of brave Wookiees that defends Kashyyyk when the Separatists invade the planet.

Q & A

How long is a Gungan's tongue?

A Gungan's tongue is over one meter long. Perfect for eating frogs raw! The Gungans' spit is so thick and sticky that it can plug holes in almost anything.

BRICK-SIZED FACT

LEGO Sebulba walks on his arms thanks to a completely custom minifigure mold.

FORCE KNOWLEDGE

EWOK ATTACK!

Don't let their furry looks fool you—these tiny terrors build catapults and gliders for battle. Some Ewoks have even been known to try to eat humans! Just ask Han Solo and Luke Skywalker, who were once captured by a tribe of Ewoks on Endor.

FORCE FACTS

Name: Sebulba

Homeworld: Malastare

Species: Dug

Occupation: Podracer

Favorite thing: Cheating!

REALLY?!

Aquatic Mon Calamari build whole cities underwater. They use tubes, like giant water slides, to travel from building to building.

ALIEN SPECIES

SOME HAVE WINGS and some have giant ears, others are furry, and lots are scaly. These are some of the galaxy's most awesome—and disgusting—aliens!

STRANGE

Geonosians use brain worms that slither up noses and turn people into zombies!

FORCE FACTS

Name: Ree-Yees

Homeworld: Kinyen

Species: Gran

Weapons: Short blaster gun

Dislikes: His boss, Jabba the Hutt

THE UNIVERSE IN UNITS

3

Eye stalks on Ree-Yees, a member of the Gran species

ALIEN CREATURES

WHETHER WANDERING the dunes of Tatooine or stalking the snowy wastes of Hoth, alien creatures make the galaxy wonderfully wild!

BRICK-SIZED FACT

The LEGO wampa is specially designed to hold a minifigure in its left hand.

FORCE FACTS

Name: Wampa

Homeworld: Hoth

Favorite food: Tauntaun legs

Weapons: Sharp teeth and claws

Known for: His messy cave

FORCE KNOWLEDGE

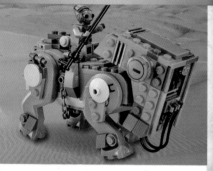

LUGGABEASTS

Luggabeasts are huge, part-robotic creatures. On Jakku, scavengers known as Teedos use them for heavy work. Luggabeasts' heads are permanently hidden beneath armor plating, and their mechanical parts give them great strength and stamina.

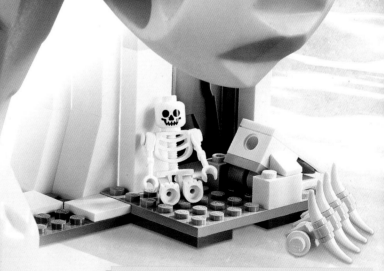

TABLE SCRAPS

The skeletons and bones of the wampa's past meals lie on the floor of his icy cave. The wampa drags his food back to the cave to devour it raw!

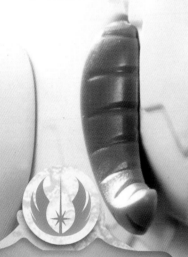

DOs AND DON'Ts FOR

RIDING A TAUNTAUN

DO...
- FEED IT TASTY TREATS
- WEAR WARM CLOTHES
- WHISPER NICE THINGS IN ITS EAR
- HOLD ON TIGHT!

DON'T...
- RIDE WITHOUT YOUR TAUNTAUN LICENSE
- GET TOO CLOSE TO A WAMPA
- RIDE DURING A SNOWSTORM
- SNIFF ITS STINKY FUR!

TOP 3
Reasons to ride a kaadu

1 **SPEED**
Their long legs allow them to move quickly through the swamps of Naboo.

2 **STRENGTH**
They can pull a wagon full of heavy energy-balls (Gungan weapons).

3 **EASE**
It's so easy, even silly Gungan Jar Jar Binks can do it!

REALLY?!
The dianoga lives on the Death Star munching on garbage, sewage, and anything unlucky enough to fall into its trash compactor!

THE UNIVERSE IN UNITS
26
Teeth on a LEGO dewback

PROTOCOL DROIDS

THEY HAVE PERFECT manners, speak millions of languages, and know almost every culture there is to know. Don't underestimate these clever protocol droids!

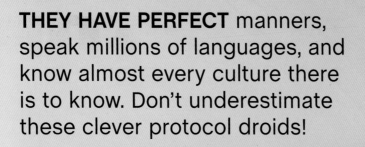

BRICK-SIZED FACT
TC-14 is the only LEGO protocol droid with a silver chrome finish.

GODLY DROID
When C-3PO meets the Ewoks, they are dazzled by his shiny gold plating. They declare him a god and carry him on a throne to their home, Bright Tree Village.

STRANGE

C-3PO's memory was erased after the Clone Wars. He forgot all of his adventures from that time.

TECH BOX

K-3PO
Not many protocol droids make it to the rank of lieutenant, but clever K-3PO is an exception. He coordinates all of the droids in the Rebel Alliance when they are stationed at Hoth Echo Base.

Processors programmed for tactical calculations

Photoreceptors for processing visual data

Vocabulator

White body paint is perfect for snowy Hoth

Rank markings of a rebel lieutenant

“WE SEEM TO BE MADE TO
SUFFER.
IT’S OUR LOT IN LIFE.”
C-3PO

TOP 3

Reasons for a protocol droid to take an oil bath

1. TO WASH AWAY CARBON SCORING AFTER A BLASTER FIGHT
2. TO REMOVE THE TATOOINE SAND BETWEEN ITS TOES
3. TO LOOSEN UP FROZEN JOINTS

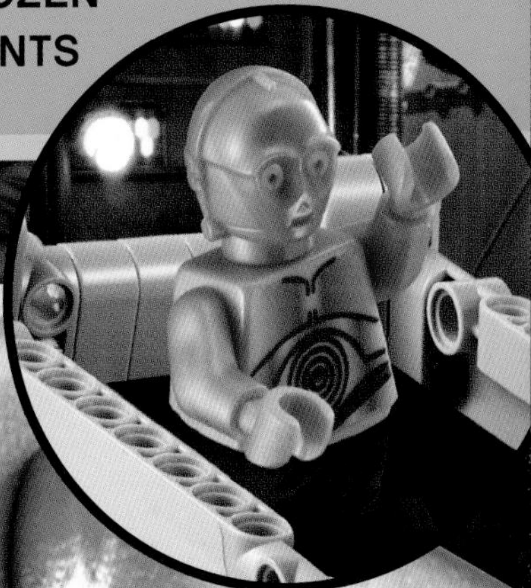

AWESOME!

C-3PO was originally built out of spare parts by nine-year-old Anakin Skywalker.

FORCE FACTS

Name: C-3PO

Affiliation: Rebel Alliance/ Resistance

Best friend: R2-D2

Languages known: Nearly 7,000,000

THE UNIVERSE IN UNITS

10,000

Chrome-gold C-3PO minifigures randomly included in LEGO *Star Wars* sets in 2007, to celebrate the 30th anniversary of *Star Wars*

ASTROMECH

THESE GALACTIC MECHANICS and navigators are a pilot's best friend. Always handy in a crisis, astromech droids beep and whistle away while saving the day!

THE UNIVERSE IN UNITS

21+

The number of handy tools R2-D2 possesses

FORCE FACTS

Name: R2-D2

Affiliation: Republic, Rebel Alliance

Species: Industrial Automaton

Best friend: C-3PO

Language: Binary code (droid language composed of electronic sounds)

BRICK-SIZED FACT

There are seven versions of the R2-D2 minifigure, including a festive snowman version!

"**THESE ASTRO DROIDS** ARE GETTING QUITE OUT OF HAND."

C-3PO

R2-D2'S DROID SKILL

BRAVERY

LOYALTY

DRINKS SERVING

DROIDS

REALLY?!

After Kylo Ren destroys Luke's efforts to train new Jedi, Luke goes into hiding, and R2-D2 shuts himself down. He has been dormant ever since.

PERFECT MATCH

R7-A7 is Jedi Padawan Ahsoka Tano's brave astromech. They are a good match—both are a little bit aggressive!

ASTROMECH SERVANT

Jabba the Hutt once made R2-D2 work on his sail barge, serving drinks to guests.

Q&A

Who is Obi-Wan Kenobi's astromech droid?

Obi-Wan works with R2-D2 on countless missions, but he really belongs to Anakin Skywalker.

R4-P17 belongs to the Jedi Order, but he works as Obi-Wan's astromech sidekick during most of the Clone Wars.

Obi-Wan was joined by another droid, R4-G9 (also known as "Geenie"), on his mission to Utapau. R4-G9 rode along in Obi-Wan's Jedi Interceptor.

AWESOME DROIDS

THEY ARE PILOTS, portable power chargers, mechanics, medics, and more. There is a robotic droid for nearly every job you can imagine!

TOP 3
Reasons why droids are the best workers

1 THEY NEVER STOP FOR LUNCH

2 THEY NEVER ASK FOR A RAISE

3 THEY CAN LEARN NEW SKILLS BY DOWNLOADING NEW PROGRAMMING

REALLY?!

Some people don't treat droids kindly. The Mos Eisley Cantina bartender doesn't allow droids to come inside because they don't buy drinks!

BRICK-SIZED FACT

The GNK droid's body is used in other LEGO sets as a mailbox!

Q & A
Which droids are good in an emergency?

2-1B is a skilled medical droid. He is programmed to perform all kinds of medical tasks, like bandaging wounds and replacing lost hands.

Surgical assistant droids help doctors to do their work, and monitor the bacta tanks in which heroes quickly heal.

HELPFUL DROIDS

GNK DROID
GNK (pronounced "gonk") droids supply power to just about anything, including other droids.

MOUSE DROID ▶
Mouse droids zoom around the halls of the Death Star and Star Destroyers, cleaning the floors as they go.

WOW!

A BB-8 droid's rolling, circular body allows it to travel at much faster speeds than most other droid models.

FORCE FACTS

Name: BB-8

Affiliation: Resistance

Owner: Poe Dameron

Droid type: Astromech

Skills: Navigation, ship maintenance, piloting, data storage

DROID KIDNAPPERS

Pesky Jawas kidnap droids and sell them to the highest bidder! The Jawa transfer crane lifts droids by their heads into their hulking sandcrawler.

SURVIVORS

THE PLANETS JAKKU AND TATOOINE are difficult places to live! They're dangerously hot, and there's little water. Strange creatures and humans survive in these desert environments by adapting in unique ways.

FORCE NUMBERS

3,296 pieces
Included in Sandcrawler (set 75059)

30kph (18.6mph)
Maximum speed of a Jawa sandcrawler

6 minifigures
Featured in Jabba's Sail Barge (set 7962), including R2-D2 with a drinks tray

3 sets
Include Jawa minifigures

FORCE KNOWLEDGE

DESERT THIEVES
Fearsome Sand People survive in the desert by raiding settlements and stealing supplies from farmers, traders, and unlucky travelers!

NO WAY!
Jawas have a reputation for being dirty and smelly. Some people believe that, underneath their hoods, Jawas look like rats.

"DISGUSTING CREATURES!"
C-3PO ABOUT JAWAS

Q&A
How do you travel in the desert?

ON THE BACK OF A DEWBACK
Dewbacks carry people and cargo on their backs. When the sun goes down, these lizards slow to a standstill.

AT TOP SPEED
Luke learned to fly by piloting a T-16 skyhopper through the canyons of Tatooine.

IN STYLE
Jabba the Hutt carries guards, slaves, and prisoners across the sand dunes aboard his personal barge.

JAKKU SCAVENGER

Rey works as a scavenger, going into spooky old starship wrecks looking for anything valuable. She works for a cruel junk dealer named Unkar Plutt, who uses his thugs to boss Rey and the other scavengers around.

STRANGE

Tatooine is so dry, citizens have to draw water from the air. Luke's Aunt Beru and Uncle Owen own a moisture farm that uses vaporators to collect water.

AWESOME!

Unkar Plutt's brutes wear scary masks to hide their identities. They aren't very smart, and Unkar mainly uses them to threaten people.

FORCE FACTS

Name: Rey

Occupation: Scavenger

Affiliation: Resistance

Species: Human

Homeworld: Jakku

Abilities: Fighting, scavenging, mechanics, the Force

BRICK-SIZED FACT

T-16 Skyhopper (set 75081) is the first set to feature a Tatooine womp rat.

THE UNIVERSE IN UNITS
846MPH
Maximum speed of a T-16 skyhopper

"FOLLOW ME!"

REY TO FINN

RENEGADES

A **RENEGADE** is a person who changes their path in life, deserting one organization to join another. There are some people in the galaxy, like Finn, whose conscience leads them to abandon evil paths for more honorable ones. Others, like Count Dooku, Pong Krell, or Anakin Skywalker, turn to the dark side.

FORCE KNOWLEDGE

JEDI PATHS

Count Dooku begins a line of Jedi with remarkable career paths. Dooku leaves the Jedi and becomes a Sith. His Padawan, Qui-Gon Jinn, is very independent. Less so is Qui-Gon's student, Obi-Wan Kenobi. Obi-Wan's Padawan, Anakin Skywalker, becomes the evil Darth Vader.

FORCE FACTS

Name: Finn

Occupation: Former stormtrooper, Resistance fighter

Affiliation: Resistance

Species: Human

Abilities: Blaster combat, lightsaber fighting

NO WAY!

Jedi General Pong Krell sends clones to their deaths without any reason—except perhaps, to please evil Darth Sidious, whom he wishes to join!

FORCE NUMBERS ●●●●

3 versions
Of the Count Dooku minifigure

2 minifigures
Wear stolen stormtrooper armor— Han Solo and Luke Skywalker

1 set
Features Pong Krell (set 75004)

TOP 3
Daring disguises

1 **LEIA ORGANA**
As Boushh the bounty hunter, Leia deceives Jabba to enter his palace and rescue Han Solo.

2 **LANDO CALRISSIAN**
Lando secretly works as one of Jabba's skiff guards to help Leia, and then Luke, escape the gangster.

3 **LUKE SKYWALKER**
Luke wears stolen stormtrooper armor to get past the Death Star security forces and rescue Leia.

FORCE KNOWLEDGE

KANAN JARRUS
When his Jedi Master, Depa Billaba, is defeated by clone troopers, Padawan Caleb Dume abandons his Jedi education. He changes his name to Kanan Jarrus and goes into hiding before eventually joining the fight against the Empire.

> **" I'VE GOT NOTHING TO FIGHT FOR. "**
>
> FINN

REALLY?!
Finn borrowed Poe's Resistance fighter jacket after the pair of them crash-landed on the planet Jakku.

FORCE NUMBERS •••●

6 sets
Feature BARC (Biker Advanced Recon Commando) speeders

4 tools/weapons
Inside Rey's Speeder set, including a buzzsaw and electrobinoculars

1m (3.3ft)
Maximum altitude Luke's landspeeder can fly

Q&A
How high can a speeder fly?

Landspeeders and speeder bikes like Kanan's tend to fly near the ground.

Airspeeders and swoop bikes can fly faster and at higher altitudes.

FORCE KNOWLEDGE

LOST JEDI
Jedi don't always know everything! When Anakin's mother is kidnapped by a tribe of warriors known as Sand People, he returns to his home planet of Tatooine to rescue her. He hasn't been home for some time, so he has to stop and ask some local Jawas for directions!

BRICK-SIZED FACT
Four versions of Luke's landspeeder have been released: 1999's Landspeeder (set 7110), 2004's Mos Eisley Cantina (4501), 2010's Luke's Landspeeder (8092), and 2014's Cantina (75052).

TOP 5
Fastest good-guy speeders

1 ANAKIN'S CUSTOM ▶ AIRSPEEDER
720kph (450mph)

2 REY'S SPEEDER - - - ▶
450kph (280mph)

3 EZRA BRIDGER'S MODIFIED 614-AVA SPEEDER BIKE ▶
375kph (233mph)

4 OWEN LARS' ZEPHYR-G SWOOP BIKE ▶
350kph (217mph)

5 LUKE'S X-34 LANDSPEEDER ▶
250kph (155mph)

HERO SPEEDERS

THE GALAXY'S GOOD GUYS are always on the move! Fortunately there is a speeder for every situation, to race heroes including Anakin, Ezra, Luke, and Rey toward the action.

BRICK-SIZED FACT

Rey's Speeder (set 75099) comes with a detachable sled for when she needs to sandsurf across the dunes, away from danger!

WORLDS OF

NO WAY!

When they first land on Endor, a group of rebels are caught in Ewok nets. Luke has to use his brain, and the Force, to save his friends.

THE GALAXY IS full of inhabited planets. People and alien creatures live in all sorts of unusual landscapes, from deserts and ice fields to cloud cities and worlds covered in water.

BESPIN

A gas planet where precious Tibanna gas is mined and processed at Cloud City.

HOTH

An icy, barren planet where the Rebel Alliance sets up Echo Base in secret.

KAMINO

A water world that is mysteriously erased from the star charts in the Jedi archives.

FORCE NUMBERS ● ● ● ●

698 bricks
Included in Cloud City (set 10123)

5,217 levels
Highest reported building height on Coruscant

17 minifigures
Featured in Ewok Village (set 10236)

13 sets
Include Gungan minifigures

2 suns
Can be seen from Tatooine

YAVIN 4

This fourth moon of the red-gas giant Yavin is home to the Rebel Alliance and its forces.

> **"THERE'S NOTHING TO SEE.**
> I USED TO LIVE HERE, YOU KNOW. **"**
>
> **LUKE SKYWALKER TO HAN SOLO**

TATOOINE

This desert world is home to the Skywalkers, as well as

WONDER

TOP 3
Biggest galactic populations

1 **1 TRILLION+**
The home of politics in the galaxy, Coruscant has a large, diverse population.

2 **100+ BILLION**
Geonosis has billions of insectoid workers for its battle droid factories.

3 **1 BILLION+**
Kamino's population grows as an army of clones is developed on the planet.

NABOO
A beautiful world full of culture and nature. It is the homeworld of Padmé, Palpatine, and the Gungans.

CORUSCANT
The capital world of the Republic and the Empire. Coruscant is almost completely covered by cities.

ENDOR AND ITS FOREST MOON
The Empire builds the second Death Star in orbit around Endor's forest moon, where the Ewoks live.

ENDOR

> " ALDERAAN IS PEACEFUL. WE HAVE **NO WEAPONS**.
>
> PRINCESS LEIA TO GRAND MOFF TARKIN

ALDERAAN
This peaceful world is the home of Princess Leia. She was raised here by Bail and Breha Organa.

FOREST MOON

DEATH STAR
That's no moon! This battle station has the power to destroy entire planets in one laser blast.

DEATH STAR

THE RESISTANCE

THE RESISTANCE WAS formed by General Leia Organa to keep watch on the activities of the mysterious First Order. She leads this group of freedom fighters in protecting the galaxy from the powers of the dark side.

BRICK-SIZED FACT
Poe's minifigure flies two different X-wing LEGO sets: a blue Resistance X-wing and his unique black and orange X-wing.

REALLY?!
Poe flies a standard blue Resistance X-wing before it is destroyed on Jakku. He later flies a customized X-wing.

STRANGE
Poe first flew a starship when he was just six years old!

RESISTANCE TROOPS

◄ SOLDIERS
The Resistance's soldiers do not have fancy armor, but they are braver than any stormtrooper.

◄ PILOTS
The Resistance's X-wing pilots are elite fliers, who take the battle to the First Order.

GROUND CREW ►
The pilots may win the glory, but they'd be stuck on the ground without the handy ship mechanics.

DROIDS ►
Many astromech droids serve bravely in the Resistance, helping pilots fly their ships.

TOP 3
Resistance leaders

1 GENERAL LEIA ORGANA
Leia puts her royal title behind her, and leaves the New Republic Senate to lead the Resistance as its general.

2 ADMIRAL STATURA
Admiral Statura serves as Leia's second-in-command. He fought in the Rebellion when he was still a teenager, and is an old friend of Leia.

3 ADMIRAL ACKBAR
Admiral Ackbar served with Leia during the Rebellion. He came out of retirement to battle the First Order.

NO WAY!
Pilot Poe Dameron's parents fought in the Rebel Alliance, so he followed in their footsteps.

FORCE FACTS
Name: Poe Dameron

Occupation: Starfighter pilot

Affiliation: Resistance

Species: Human

Homeworld: Yavin 4

Personal idol: General Leia Organa

X-WINGS

X-WING STARFIGHTERS MAY be small in size, but that doesn't mean they aren't dangerous! Sleek and speedy, X-wings are the starfighter of choice for the Rebel Alliance. Decades later, the Resistance upgrades to the T-70 X-wing and battles the First Order!

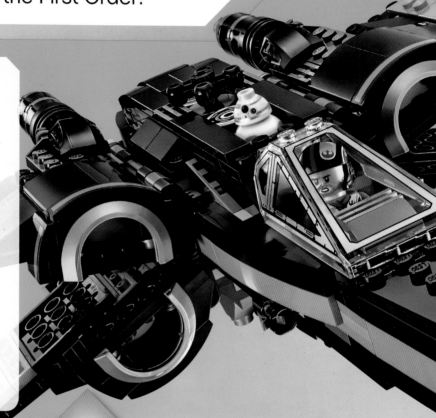

FORCE NUMBERS

1,559 bricks
Found in the Red Five X-wing Starfighter (set 10240)

1050kph (652mph)
The X-wing's maximum speed

13 versions
Of the X-wing pilot minifigure

2 torpedo launchers
On each X-wing

1 astromech droid
Required to copilot an X-wing

THE UNIVERSE IN UNITS
53,350,200
The number of bricks required to build a life-sized LEGO X-wing

WHO'S WHO IN THE HANGAR

POE DAMERON

Poe is the best pilot in the Resistance. His parents were both veterans of the old Rebel Alliance.

LUKE SKYWALKER ▶

This Jedi learned his amazing piloting skills from targeting womp rats in his T-16 on Tatooine.

◀ WEDGE ANTILLES

X-wing pilot Wedge is a true hero. He displays his amazing piloting skills in three huge battles—Yavin, Hoth, and Endor.

BIGGS DARKLIGHTER ▶

Luke's childhood friend from Tatooine attends the Imperial Acedemy but soon joins the Rebellion.

◀ JEK PORKINS

This brave rebel pilot flies alongside Luke at the Battle of Yavin, and helps destroy the Death Star's turbolaser.

BRICK-SIZED FACT

In May 2013, the LEGO Group unveiled a life-sized LEGO X-wing model in Times Square, New York to celebrate the launch of the animated TV series *The Yoda Chronicles*.

DOs AND DON'Ts FOR

X-WING GROUND CREW

DO...

- HAVE A HOT CUP OF SPIRAN CAF READY FOR YOUR PILOT IN THE MORNING
- KEEP R2-D2 AND BB-8 WELL-OILED AND FULLY CHARGED
- CLEAN THE DAGOBAH MUD AND PESTS OUT OF LUKE'S X-WING

DON'T...

- TAKE SECRET NAPS IN THE PILOT COCKPIT
- LEAVE TOOLS AROUND TO TRIP UP DROIDS
- BORROW THE X-WING AND GO FOR A RIDE

POE'S SHIP

Poe flies a unique, customized X-wing, code-named *Black One*. It is coated in a special paint that helps to hide the ship from enemy sensors.

REBEL SHIPS

THE REBEL ALLIANCE may not have as many ships as the mighty Empire, but the rebel pilots' bravery and skill more than make up for this!

TOP 3
Space battles between the Empire and the rebels

1 **BATTLE OF YAVIN**
The first Death Star is destroyed by the Rebel Alliance as it approaches their base on the moon Yavin 4.

2 **BATTLE OF ENDOR**
Above the forest moon of Endor, the Death Star II is demolished by General Lando Calrissian aboard the *Millennium Falcon*.

3 **BATTLE OF JAKKU**
A year after Endor, the rebels further cripple the Empire by defeating a huge Imperial fleet above the desert planet Jakku.

REALLY?!
A-wings are among the first ships used by the rebels—but they are difficult to fly because they have no room for an astromech copilot.

FORCE NUMBERS ● ● ● ●

1,487 bricks
In the B-wing Starfighter (set 10227)

1,300kph (808mph)
The A-wing's maximum speed

4 sets
Feature minifigure-scale A-wings

NO WAY!
Anakin Skywalker has piloted a Y-wing ship many times, but as Darth Vader, he destroys them with his TIE advanced starfighter.

STRANGE

The B-wing starfighter was designed by a Mon Calamari named Quarrie. His species lives in watery environments, and he doesn't even like to fly!

REBEL STARFIGHTERS

Rebel starfighters are vital to the Rebel Alliance in winning its many battles against the Empire. Each starfighter is named after the letter of the alphabet that it resembles.

A-WING

B-WING

Y-WING

X-WING

> " I WILL **FINISH** WHAT YOU STARTED. "
> KYLO REN TO DARTH VADER'S CHARRED HELMET

FORCE FACTS

Name: Kylo Ren

Occupation: Dark side warrior, Knight of Ren

Affiliation: First Order

Species: Human

Homeworld: Unknown

Abilities: Lightsaber skills, dark side Force user

DARTH SIDIOUS

Sith Lord Darth Sidious always seems to be looking for a new apprentice! He wants to be sure he has the best available.

DARTH MAUL

Sidious' first apprentice is a Zabrak who wields a double-bladed lightsaber. He is defeated by Obi-Wan Kenobi.

COUNT DOOKU

A former Jedi, secretly known as Darth Tyranus, Dooku leads the Separatist Alliance. He is eventually defeated in a lightsaber duel with Yoda.

DARTH VADER

The apprentice that Sidious thought he always wanted—but when Vader's son Luke is discovered, Sidious considers another upgrade...

SHUTTLES

WHEN BAD GUYS TRAVEL, they want three things: security, speed, and style. So it's no surprise that the shuttles of the Separatists, Empire, and First Order are the best that credits can buy!

DOs AND DON'Ts FOR A SHUTTLE PILOT

DO...

- FLY IN CASUAL ATTIRE
- CHECK FOR TRACKING DEVICES
- KEEP YOUR CLEARANCE CODES UP-TO-DATE

DON'T...

- KEEP SITH PASSENGERS WAITING
- ASK FOR DIRECTIONS
- LET EWOKS INSIDE THE COCKPIT

UPSILON-CLASS SHUTTLE

Kylo Ren uses this First Order command shuttle to travel between ships and planetary surfaces. It has huge wings and powerful twin laser cannons.

66

> ## "ALERT MY STAR DESTROYER TO PREPARE FOR MY ARRIVAL."
> DARTH VADER

LAMBDA-CLASS SHUTTLE
Elegant and reliable, this is the preferred transport for officers and high-ranking officials associated with the Empire.

SENTINEL-CLASS SHUTTLE
A common sight in the Outer Rim of the galaxy, the *Sentinel* is mostly used for transporting troops.

THETA-CLASS SHUTTLE
Only the most important politicians, like Emperor Palpatine, use the *Theta*-class shuttle.

SHEATHIPEDE-CLASS SHUTTLE
This Separatist shuttle ferries allies of the Republic, like the Nemoidian Nute Gunray, to their sinister appointments.

THE
FIRST ORDER

THE SINISTER FIRST ORDER has risen from the ruins of the defeated Empire. Led by the mysterious Supreme Leader Snoke and the dark warrior Kylo Ren, these vile villains are plotting to conquer the galaxy.

NO WAY!

The First Order has built a superweapon even more powerful than the Old Empire's Death Stars—the Starkiller.

FIRST ORDER **LEADERS**

◀ **KYLO REN**
A dark side warrior who acts as the First Order's enforcer.

◀ **CAPTAIN PHASMA**
A chrome-armor-wearing commander who leads the First Order's stormtroopers.

◀ **GENERAL HUX**
A young, ruthless officer in charge of the Starkiller superweapon program.

DOs AND DON'Ts FOR

BEING IN THE FIRST ORDER

DO...
- FOLLOW CAPTAIN PHASMA'S ORDERS
- IRON YOUR UNIFORM
- SPEAK ONLY WHEN SPOKEN TO

DON'T...
- QUESTION AUTHORITY
- RUN AWAY
- ANNOY KYLO REN

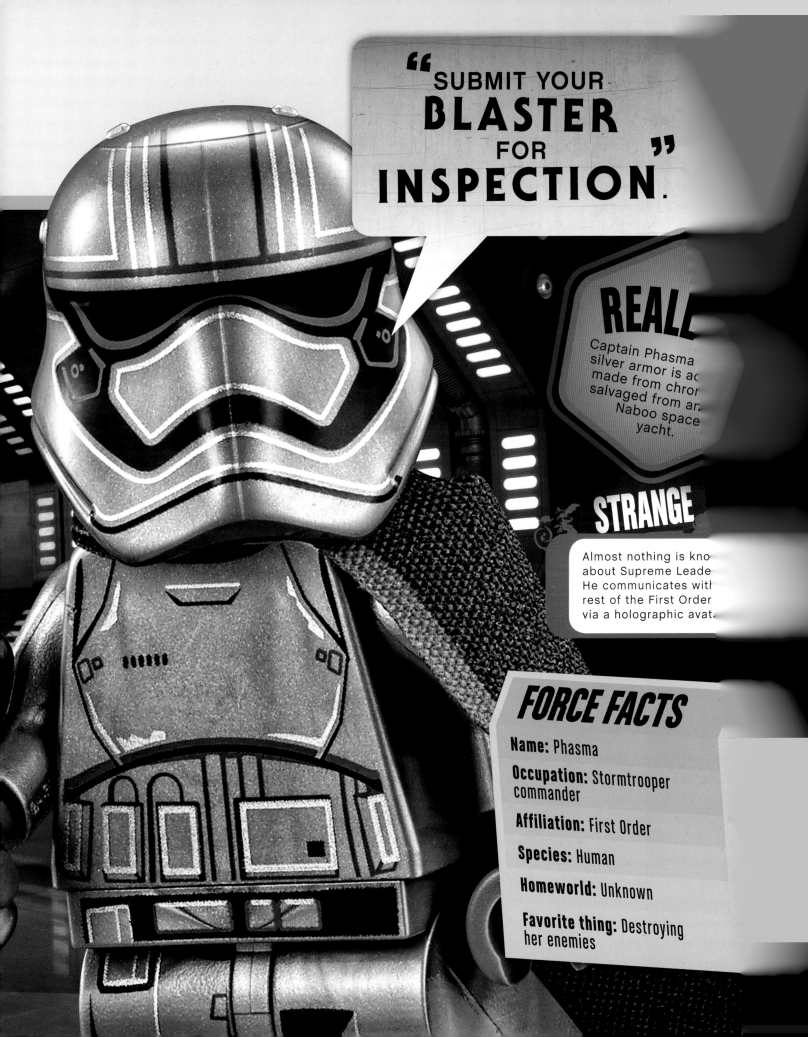

OFFICERS

AUTHORITY, EXPERTISE, and dedication: that's what it takes to be an officer in the galaxy. These galactic leaders won't take no for an answer!

FORCE REPORT

OVERCONFIDENT OFFICER

Once an officer in the Republic, Grand Moff Tarkin rose through the Imperial ranks to become an officer and commander of the Death Star. Tarkin's arrogance is his downfall. Rather than evacuate the Death Star, he underestimates the rebels and stays aboard the station when Luke Skywalker destroys it.

BRICK-SIZED FACT

The First Order officers share similar colors to the Imperial officer minifigures, but they feature unique hats, insignia, and uniform designs.

REALLY?!

Imperial officers who are loyal to the military look down on self-serving bounty hunters like Bossk.

TOP 4
Worst jobs for an officer

1 **CLEANING THE TRASH COMPACTOR**
This dirty garbage pit is impossible to get clean.

FORCE KNOWLEDGE

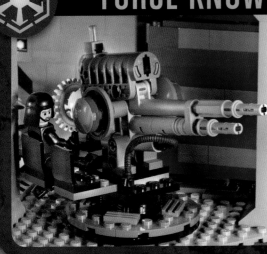

TURBOLASER CANNON

Highly trained Death Star troopers manage to shoot down rebel X-wing pilots during the Battle of Yavin. Their cannon blasts can take down much larger ships, too.

THE UNIVERSE IN UNITS

24

Minifigures included in the LEGO Death Star set

IMPERIAL GUARD

These silent soldiers in red armor are skilled warriors who guard the most important person in the Empire: the Emperor himself!

FORCE FACTS

Name: Hux

Occupation: General

Affiliation: First Order

Species: Human

Homeworld: Arkanis

Pet hate: Kylo Ren telling him what to do

> **" YOU HAVE FAILED ME FOR THE LAST TIME, ADMIRAL. "**
>
> DARTH VADER TO ADMIRAL OZZEL

 CHASING DROIDS ON TATOOINE

Somehow, you can never find the droids you are looking for.

 SERVING ON THE DEATH STAR

No matter how many times you try, rebels always find a way to blow up your battle station.

 MEETINGS WITH DARTH VADER

He just doesn't like to be questioned, okay?

STORMTROOPERS

STORMTROOPERS ARE the foot soldiers of the Empire. These white-armored warriors are trained to obey orders without question. Years after the Empire is defeated by the Rebel Alliance, the First Order begins training a new generation of stormtroopers.

BRICK-SIZED FACT

A total of four "full-sized" LEGO AT-ATs have been released, including 2007's motorized, walking AT-AT (set 10178), which stands over 12in (30cm) high.

HEIGHT CHART

IMPERIAL WALKERS

The Empire employs enormous walking machines—known as "walkers"—to terrify its enemies during battle. The walkers are driven by specially trained troopers.

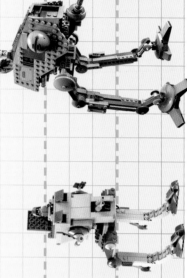

AT-AT
Enormous all-terrain walker

AT-DP
Common patrol walker

AT-ST
Speedy scout walker

12in (30cm)

8in (20cm)

4in (10cm)

FIRST ORDER
TROOPER TYPES

▶ **CAPTAIN PHASMA**
Captain Phasma leads the First Order's stormtroopers. She is a ruthless commander and deadly warrior.

STORMTROOPER ▶
These are the foot soldiers of the First Order, and the first to respond to Resistance activity.

▼ **STORMTROOPER OFFICER**
Supervising officers wear an orange pauldron on their shoulder. They manage ground troops and report to Captain Phasma.

▶ **FLAMETROOPERS**
These specialist stormtroopers are armed with powerful cannons that fire out jets of burning gel.

"MOVE ALONG... MOVE ALONG."

STORMTROOPER

REALLY?!

Stormtroopers identify themselves by ID numbers—but rebels just call them "bucket-heads!"

THE UNIVERSE IN UNITS

38,000

Troopers assigned to Darth Vader's ship, the *Executor*

BLASTER FIRE

Stormtroopers are armed with powerful E-11 blasters. They fire three types of energy beams: sting (yellow), stun (blue rings), and lethal (red).

FORCE NUMBERS

1,138 bricks

Included in the AT-AT set (75054), operated by stormtroopers

14 sets

Include snowtroopers

13 years

After the Clone Army is born, it is replaced by the Stormtrooper Corps

12 versions

Of the stormtrooper minifigure

3 troopers

Is the minimum crew required to drive an AT-AT walker

TROOPER HISTORY

CLONE TROOPERS ORIGINALLY fought for the Republic—but they changed sides at the end of the Clone Wars. Since then, the Empire's soldiers have been known as stormtroopers.

TOP 3
Clone trooper blasters

1 **DC-15A BLASTER**
Short-range blaster pistol issued to all clone troopers. It has a 500-shot cartridge.

2 **DC-15 BLASTER RIFLE**
Standard long-range weapon. Can fire at battle droids 500 times without reloading.

3 **DC-17 REPEATER HAND BLASTER**
The preferred blaster pistol of clone leaders, such as Captain Rex, Commander Fox, and Commander Cody. It has a 50-shot capacity.

NO WAY!
At the end of the Clone Wars, Darth Sidious gave a secret command, known as Order 66. This directed the clone troopers to suddenly attack their Jedi generals!

THE EVOLUTION OF... STORMTROOPERS

PHASE I CLONE TROOPER
The clone troopers were all cloned from one man: the bounty hunter Jango Fett. Clone trooper armor was based on Jango's armor.

PHASE II CLONE TROOPER
By the end of the Clone Wars, the armor was much stronger. Some battalions customized their armor with their own colors and emblems.

IMPERIAL STORMTROOPER
No longer clones, now stormtroopers are human volunteers. They are a mixed bunch—some are better than others!

FIRST ORDER STORMTROOPER
The highly trained troopers of the First Order wear advanced armor and carry powerful weapons.

FORCE FACTS

Name: Captain Rex

Affiliation: The Galactic Republic

Species: Human clone

Homeworld: Kamino

Abilities: Leadership, combat, battle strategy

REALLY?!

Captain Rex is proud to be a clone trooper. He keeps track of the enemies he has destroyed by marking up a tally on his helmet.

HOW TO TALK LIKE A...
CLONE TROOPER

"Shinies"
New clone cadets with shiny new armor

"Clankers"
Battle droids

"Droid poppers"
Grenades that shut down battle droids

"Buzzers"
Flying platforms that transport battle droids

"Rollers"
Hailfire droids, which roll on huge wheel treads

"Rollies"
Droideka droids, which curl into a ball and roll

REALLY?!

In their younger years, clone troopers grow and age at approximately twice the rate of normal human beings!

THE UNIVERSE IN UNITS
1,200,000
Active clone soldiers at the start of the Clone Wars

DARK WORLDS

PLANETS THEMSELVES are not evil, but they can be the scene of dark deeds of the Sith—the Empire, the First Order, and their dark servants...

WHERE DO PALPATINE AND HIS SERVANTS FALL?

 Darth Maul is cut in half by Obi-Wan Kenobi on **NABOO**. (Amazingly, the Sith survives!)

Jango Fett is defeated by Mace Windu on **GEONOSIS**.

 Count Dooku falls in battle with Anakin Skywalker above **CORUSCANT**.

Vicious General Grievous is destroyed by Obi-Wan Kenobi on **UTAPAU**.

 Savage Opress is defeated by Darth Sidious in an epic duel on **MANDALORE**.

The Inquisitor falls to his doom above **MUSTAFAR**, rather than face Vader's wrath for not defeating the rebels.

 Grand Moff Tarkin is aboard the Death Star when it is destroyed at the Battle of **YAVIN**.

Darth Vader destroys Emperor Palpatine and sacrifices himself above **ENDOR** to save his son, Luke Skywalker.

DOs AND DON'TS ON MUSTAFAR

DO...
- TAKE A RIDE ON A GIANT LAVA FLEA
- SURF THE LAVA FLOWS
- COOK HOT DOGS

DON'T...
- BRING YOUR HEAVY HOTH SNOW GEAR
- GET IN A LIGHTSABER DUEL WITH OBI-WAN
- STAND ON WOBBLY STRUCTURES HANGING OVER LAVA POOLS

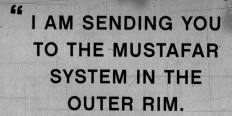

" I AM SENDING YOU TO THE MUSTAFAR SYSTEM IN THE OUTER RIM. **YOU WILL BE SAFE THERE.**"

GENERAL GRIEVOUS TO NUTE GUNRAY

THE UNIVERSE IN UNITS
20,000+
Estimated native population living on fiery Mustafar

FORCE NUMBERS

282 bricks
Included in Ultimate Lightsaber Duel (set 7257), based on the epic battle between Anakin and Obi-Wan on Mustafar

1 set
Features Chancellor Palpatine's Office (set 9526), based on the Chancellor's arrest on Coruscant

0%
Surface water on Mustafar

IMPORTANT EVENTS ON
Mustafar

1 CHILDREN OF THE FORCE
Palpatine hires bounty hunter Cad Bane to kidnap Force-sensitive children and hide them here.

2 SEPARATISTS' DOOM
Under orders from his new Sith Master Darth Sidious, Anakin eliminates the Separatist Alliance leaders hiding there.

3 THE END OF ANAKIN ▶
Anakin duels with his former Master, Obi-Wan... and loses!

4 KANAN IMPRISONED
Jedi Kanan Jarrus is interrogated aboard Grand Moff Tarkin's star destroyer, the *Sovereign*, in orbit.

5 REBEL VICTORY
The rebels destroy Tarkin's Star Destroyer. Luckily for the Grand Moff, he survives the explosion.

AWESOME!
The planet Umbaran, home to Separatist soldiers, is always in darkness. The Umbarans can see ultraviolet light—they see very well in the dark!

EVIL
SPEEDERS

THE SITH AND OTHER followers of the dark side are always in a hurry to carry out their horrible deeds. There are Jedi to chase, rebels to crush, and the Resistance to oppose. And for this, they need some super-fast speeders!

WOW!

Snow speeders have special heaters built into their seats to keep snowtroopers toasty warm on the icy surface of the Starkiller superweapon.

TOP 3
Fastest Sith speeders

BRICK-SIZED FACT
There are five versions of Darth Maul's *Bloodfin* speeder. Sith Infiltrator sets include four, and a simpler version comes with 1999's Lightsaber Duel (set 7101).

1 DARTH MAUL'S *BLOODFIN* SPEEDER BIKE
650kph (404mph)

2 COUNT DOOKU'S *FLITKNOT* SPEEDER
634kph (393mph)

3 GENERAL GRIEVOUS' TSMEU-6 WHEEL BIKE
330kph (205mph)

REALLY?!
General Grievous' bike isn't a normal speeder because it rolls on the ground, but neither is the varactyl, Boga, that Obi-Wan uses to chase him on Utapau.

TROOPER SPEEDERS

IMPERIAL 614-AvA SPEEDER BIKE

This bike is equipped with two blaster cannons on the front for Imperial pilots and stormtroopers to take down rebels!

IMPERIAL 74-Z SPEEDER BIKE

Used by scout troopers, this bike has a super-powerful boost that allows it to travel long distances in a short amount of time.

IMPERIAL 74-Z SNOW SPEEDER BIKE

Special steering vanes on the front of this snow speeder help the snowtroopers to track down rebels in super-quick time on snowy planets like Hoth.

FIRST ORDER SNOW SPEEDER

First Order snow speeders are bigger, fancier, and more lethal than the rest. They are equipped with rapid-fire blasters, too. The Resistance had better watch out!

FORCE NUMBERS ● ● ● ●

1000m (3281ft)
Firing range of 614-AvA speeder-bike blasters

249 bricks
Make up General Grievous' TSMEU-6 Wheel Bike (set 75040)

2 sets
Feature General Grievous' wheel bike

3 snowtroopers
Fit inside a First Order snow speeder

BAD DROIDS

BEWARE THESE bad droids! Sith and Imperial droids are designed to follow evil orders. Deadly, determined, and sometimes a little dumb, they will stop at nothing to complete a mission.

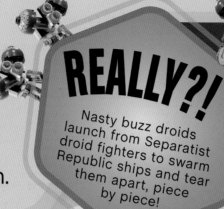

REALLY?!

Nasty buzz droids launch from Separatist droid fighters to swarm Republic ships and tear them apart, piece by piece!

FORCE NUMBERS ● ● ● ●

1,500 droid starfighters
Aboard Trade Federation battleships

20+ kinds
Of B1 battle droids

6 sets
Contain assassin droids

4 elements
Make up a standard super battle droid minifigure

DOs AND DON'Ts FOR

BAD DROID BEHAVIOR

DO...
- OBEY WITHOUT QUESTION
- DESTROY THE REPUBLIC
- WIN AT ALL COSTS

DON'T...
- WORRY ABOUT YOURSELF
- SHOW MERCY TO REBELS
- SURRENDER

SEPARATIST BATTLE DROIDS

◄ B1 BATTLE DROIDS
They may lack skill but when there are millions of battle droids rushing towards you, skill doesn't really come into it!

TACTICAL DROIDS ►
More brains than brawn, these tactical droids serve as commanding officers for the other, not-so-clever, droids.

SUPER BATTLE DROIDS ▲
Not only do super battle droids look terrifying, they are also bigger, stronger, and smarter than most standard droids.

BRICK-SIZED FACT

There is a 567-piece Destroyer Droid (set 8002) that rolls and unfurls into its attack position when spun across the floor!

DERANGED DROID

Jabba the Hutt's new droid recruits report to the evil EV-9D9 at Jabba's palace. Unfortunately for the newbies, the demented droid loves to see them suffer and she has even been known to torture them!

28
Elements in a droideka droid

FORCE FACTS

Droid Type: Commando droid

Occupation: Soldier

Affiliation: Separatist Alliance

Homeworld: Manufactured on Geonosis

Abilities: Keeping secrets

Q&A
which bad droids work for which bad guys?

A4-D is General Grievous' personal doctor droid. He is constantly having to fix Grievous' broken parts.

Pilot droid FA-4 is stuck being Count Dooku's personal pilot aboard his solar sailer starship.

DRK-1 probe droid works for Darth Maul, scouting targets and hunting down Jedi.

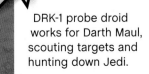

DARK SIDE
WEAPONS AND TECHNOLOGY

THE ULTIMATE GOAL of the dark side is absolute power! The Sith have developed dangerous technology to destroy their enemies and conquer the galaxy.

TOP 4
Secondary weaponry of the Death Star II

1 **768** tractor-beam emplacements

2 **30,000** turbo laser batteries

3 **7,500** laser cannons

4 **5,000** ion cannons

DOUBLE DEATH STARS
The first Death Star was destroyed by Luke Skywalker during the Battle of Yavin. However, even before that, power-hungry Chancellor Palpatine had ordered the construction of the second Death Star.

" **NOW WITNESS THE**
FIREPOWER
OF THIS FULLY ARMED AND OPERATIONAL
BATTLE STATION."
EMPEROR PALPATINE TO LUKE SKYWALKER

WOW!
Each version of the Death Star has had one big weakness: its main reactor! If something penetrates the reactor, like a lightsaber or a torpedo, the whole superweapon will blow!

FIRST ORDER WEAPONS

◀ **MEGABLASTER**
The First Order snow speeder is armed with a huge cannon known as a megablaster.

FLAMETHROWER ▲
Flametroopers carry these unusual weapons. They are guaranteed to get enemies hot under the collar!

BLASTER RIFLE ▶

Most First Order stormtroopers carry the ever-reliable F-11D blaster rifle.

SHIP **WEAPONRY**

◀ INQUISITOR TIE FIGHTER

This advanced TIE fighter, which belongs to Jedi-hunter the Inquisitor, has two laser cannons.

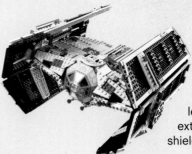

◀ TIE ADVANCED

Darth Vader always gets the best ships. His lethal starfighter has extra large wings to shield it from enemy fire.

TIE INTERCEPTOR ▶

Upgraded cannons and blasters on each of its wingtips help make this TIE a major threat at the Battle of Endor.

TIE BOMBER ▶

The fearsome TIE bomber is loaded with explosive cargo. It has dual hulls—one of which stores missile launchers.

REALLY?!

Sometimes Imperial ships get infested with pests. Worms squirm through the electronics, affecting their weapons and technology.

FORCE FACTS

Name: *Scimitar*

Model: Sith Infiltrator

Known owners: Darth Maul and Darth Sidious

Manufacturer: Republic Sienar Systems

TECHNOLOGICAL WONDER

Darth Maul's Sith Infiltrator is one of the most technologically advanced ships in the galaxy. All of it goes unnoticed, though, because few people have ever seen the ship! That's because it has a cloaking device that can make it invisible.

GANGSTERS

HUTT CRIME FAMILIES control many worlds in the Outer Rim. Greedy gangster Jabba the Hutt is worst of all—he causes big problems for Han Solo and his friends!

> " IF I TOLD YOU HALF THE THINGS I'VE HEARD ABOUT THIS **JABBA THE HUTT**, YOU'D PROBABLY SHORT CIRCUIT. "
>
> C-3PO TO R2-D2

THE UNIVERSE IN UNITS

568

Jabba's age when Anakin Skywalker leaves Tatooine to train as a Jedi

JABBA'S GANG

BIB FORTUNA
If you want to enter Jabba's palace, you have to get past his assistant first. Bib wears a metal chestplate to protect him against Jedi attacks.

REE-YEES
This Gran alien is in charge of looking after Jabba's smaller pets. He secretly hates Jabba and can't wait to escape.

MALAKILI
Animal lover Malakili used to work in a circus, taming beasts. Now he takes care of Jabba's vicious rancor—he loves the angry beast dearly!

KITHABA
This assassin guards Jabba's skiffs and sail barge. He keeps an eye on Jabba's prisoners and watches out for surprise attacks.

MAX REBO
Jabba's favorite band leader plays the keyboard to entertain the Hutt in his palace. Ortolan Max doesn't do it for the money—he gets paid in food!

JABBA'S PALACE
Jabba's palace is nestled deep inside an old B'omarr monastery. It's always full of gangsters, entertainers, bad droids, strange creatures, and a few unlucky prisoners.

TECH BOX

Decorative sails provide shade ——————

JABBA'S SAIL BARGE

Jabba's sail barge, the *Khetanna*, is a pleasure ship, but Jabba uses it for nasty business, too. He transports his prisoners into the desert on it, then feeds them to a hungry Sarlacc monster!

Double laser cannon ——————

Grate above spacious kitchen ——————

—— Steering vane

—— Jabba's throne in main compartment

—— Viewport hatch

REALLY?!

Jabba's Weequay guards can communicate without speaking. They "talk" to each other using pheromones (smells).

THE EVOLUTION OF...

GAMORREAN GUARDS

GRAY-ARMED GUARD
The 2003 variant of Jabba's porky guard has a single green head-and-torso piece.

BROWN-ARMED BRUISER
The 2006 variant has a new mold and brown arms. He carries a deadly vibro-ax.

FANCY FIGHTER
A mold with more colors highlights all of the guard's gruesome features in 2012.

FORCE NUMBERS ● ● ● ●

850 bricks
In Jabba's Sail Barge (set 6210)

9–12 years old
Approximate age of Rotta (Jabba's son) during the Clone Wars

10 minifigures
Included in Jabba's palace (set 9516)

4 sets
Include Jabba the Hutt

85

WITH SO MANY wanted men and women roaming the galaxy, bounty hunters are always busy tracking down their next target... and reward!

BOUNTY HUNTERS

FORCE KNOWLEDGE

SLAVE I
Boba Fett inherits *Slave I* from his father, Jango, and uses it to patrol the galaxy in search of bounties. It is equipped with missile launchers in case anyone tries to give him any trouble!

BRICK-SIZED FACT
Jango Fett's WESTAR-34 blasters are also used as cowboy revolvers in LEGO sets.

REALLY?!
Poor Boba Fett falls into the Sarlacc pit. Unluckily for him, it takes 1,000 years for the Sarlacc to digest its food!

FORCE FACTS
Name: Boba Fett

Affiliation: Self-employed

Frequent customer: Jabba the Hutt

Biggest bounty: Han Solo

Last seen: In the Sarlacc pit (fate unknown)

FACE CHANGE

Zam Wessel is a Clawdite shape shifter. She can change her appearance to look like almost anyone!

THE UNIVERSE IN UNITS

9

Bounty hunter droid IG-88 is built from nine LEGO bricks, including his blaster

FORCE FACTS

Name: Cad Bane

Affiliation: The highest bidder

Frequent customer: Darth Sidious

Favorite gadget: Boot rockets for flying

CAD'S BOUNTY HUNTER SKILLS

BLASTERS

FIGHTING JEDI

EVADING CAPTURE

DOs AND DON'Ts FOR

HIRING A BOUNTY HUNTER

DO...

- GIVE A GOOD DESCRIPTION OF THE TARGET
- ONLY USE REPUTABLE BOUNTY HUNTERS
- PAY THEM ON TIME

DON'T....

- ASK TOO MANY QUESTIONS
- TRY TO SHOOT THEIR BLASTERS
- CHANGE YOUR MIND

SITH SHIPS

AS IF DARK-SIDERS weren't bad enough, with their evil plots and fiery red lightsabers, they move around the galaxy on these menacing ships, too!

SOLAR SAILER

Count Dooku's solar sailer uses solar-powered sails that help it achieve great speeds during space travel.

TECH BOX

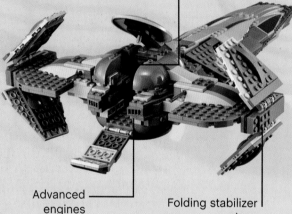

Cargo hold for spying probe droids and speeder bike

Advanced engines

Folding stabilizer wings

SITH INFILTRATOR

The Sith Infiltrator is Darth Maul's personal starship. Known as the *Scimitar*, it has advanced features and technology, including sensors and tracking devices. Its wings can fold down when it enters landing mode, and up again to make the ship aerodynamic for flight.

YOUR SOLAR SAILER IS VERY BEAUTIFUL.

IT'S A PRETTY RARE SHIP.

VERY EXPENSIVE. "

HONDO OHNAKA ON COUNT DOOKU'S SOLAR SAILER

BRICK-SIZED FACT

The Sith Infiltrator has been released in LEGO form six times between 1999 and 2015, including two mini versions.

IMPERIAL STAR DESTROYER

The dagger-like profile of this warship tells the galaxy that it's not to be messed with in a space battle! It has the power to conquer entire star systems.

2

First Order TIE pilots command a single Special Forces TIE fighter

FORCE FACTS

Name: First Order TIE Pilot

Skills: Flying starfighters, taking orders

Ship: Special Forces TIE fighter

Favorite colors: Black and red

SPECIAL FORCES TIE

Compared to the standard TIE, the Special Forces TIE fighter has enhanced engines, weapons, and sensor systems, as well as a rear-firing turret and gunner.

REALLY?!

The First Order takes much better care of its TIE pilots than the Empire did. Their ships have finally been given defensive shields.

MORE BAD GUYS

THE JEDI ARE UNDER constant threat of attack. Pesky pirates, devious cyborgs, and cunning clones go about their wicked business throughout the galaxy, causing pain and destruction everywhere.

BRICK-SIZED FACT

Tasu Leech shares the same style hair as Jedi Master Qui-Gon Jinn.

STRANGE

General Grievous chose to swap parts of his own body for robotic limbs, all so that he could be better in battle!

FORCE FACTS

Name: General Grievous

Affiliation: Separatists

Boss: Darth Sidious

Main enemy: Obi-Wan Kenobi

Pet hate: Being called a droid

TASU LEECH

Tasu Leech is the leader of the scruffy Kanjiklub gang. This group of bandits is always on the lookout for people to rob and ships to steal.

> " **BUT YOU KNOW WHAT I ALWAYS SAY: SPEAK SOFTLY AND DRIVE A BIG TANK.** "
>
> PIRATE HONDO OHNAKA

REALLY?!

Pirates like Turk Faso can't be trusted. Faso attempts to steal from his boss Hondo in order to make more profit for himself.

FORCE KNOWLEDGE

JEK-14

Jek-14 is an evil clone who is given Force powers by Count Dooku. More powerful than even Master Yoda, Jek-14 is like no other Force user. He wears custom clone armor and his left arm is made of pure energy!

TURK FASO

Turk thinks he's the real tough guy of the gang. He answers to Hondo, but doesn't think much of his pirate-management skills.

SHAHAN ALAMA

Shahan used to be part of the Weequay gang, but was asked to leave for being too nasty! Now he works alone as a bounty hunter.

HONDO OHNAKA

Leader of the terrifying Weequay pirates, fearsome Hondo roams the galaxy causing mischief with the rest of his gang.

91

DARK SIDE
POPULATIONS

THERE AREN'T ENOUGH dark-siders to take over the galaxy by themselves. Luckily for the bad guys, there are plenty of resourceful populations willing to assist in their evil plans!

AWESOME!
The Geonosian cannon shoots powerful shockwaves that can knock out multiple Jedi at once!

FORCE KNOWLEDGE

DEATH STAR PLANS

The Geonosians aren't just good at building battle droids. They created a plan for the ultimate dark side weapon—the Death Star. The plans are so secret, Poggle keeps them with him at all times!

PALPATINE'S PUPPETS

Evil General Palpatine tricks many planets into helping him take over the galaxy. The crafty Geonosians and sneaky Neimoidians are always willing to help a bad cause!

REALLY?!
Insect-like Geonosians live in hives. The warriors will freely sacrifice themselves for the good of the hive.

THE UNIVERSE IN UNITS
1.1 million
Battle droids manufactured by Geonosian workers

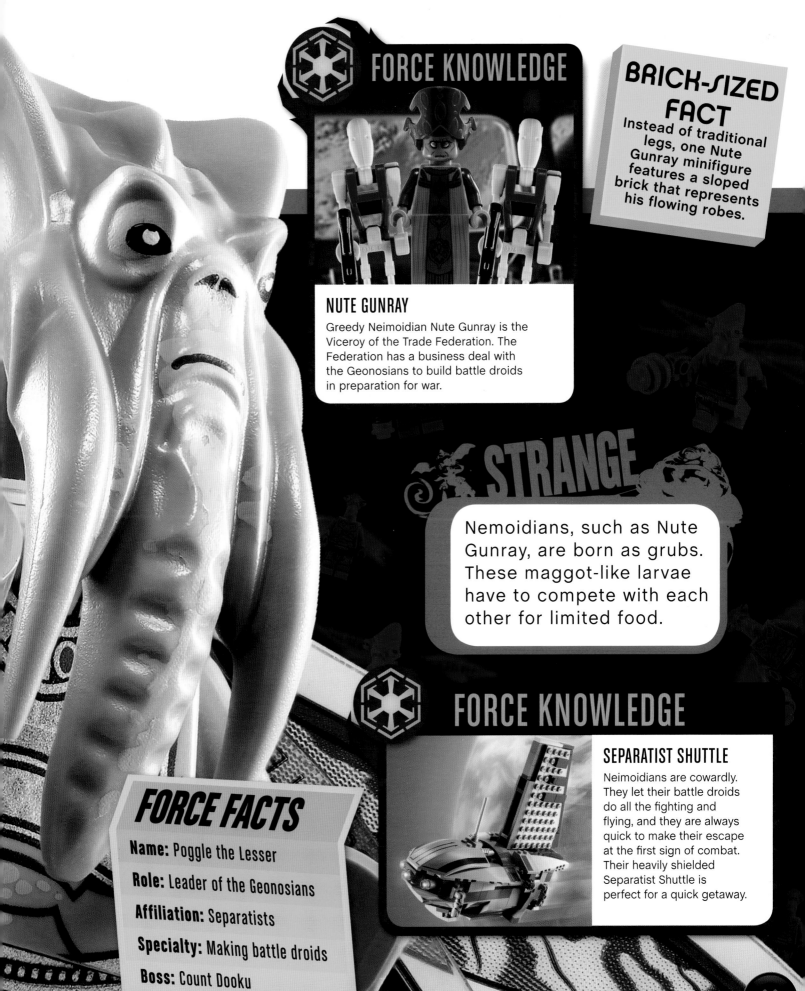

BRICK-SIZED FACT

Instead of traditional legs, one Nute Gunray minifigure features a sloped brick that represents his flowing robes.

NUTE GUNRAY

Greedy Neimoidian Nute Gunray is the Viceroy of the Trade Federation. The Federation has a business deal with the Geonosians to build battle droids in preparation for war.

STRANGE

Nemoidians, such as Nute Gunray, are born as grubs. These maggot-like larvae have to compete with each other for limited food.

FORCE KNOWLEDGE

SEPARATIST SHUTTLE

Neimoidians are cowardly. They let their battle droids do all the fighting and flying, and they are always quick to make their escape at the first sign of combat. Their heavily shielded Separatist Shuttle is perfect for a quick getaway.

FORCE FACTS

Name: Poggle the Lesser

Role: Leader of the Geonosians

Affiliation: Separatists

Specialty: Making battle droids

Boss: Count Dooku

93

BATTLE DROID
A Separatist robot designed for combat.

BOUNTY HUNTER
Someone who is hired to track down or destroy people or objects for money.

CHANCELLOR
The title given to the head of the Republic.

CHOSEN ONE
A person spoken of in an old Jedi prophecy who will bring balance to the Force.

CLONE TROOPERS
Soldiers of the Republic Clone Army. They are identical because they share the same genes.

CLONE WARS
A series of galaxy-wide battles fought between the Republic's Clone Army and the Separatist Droid Army, which took place between 22 and 19 BBY.

CYBORG
A being that is partly a living organism and partly a robot.

DARK SIDE
The evil side of the Force that feeds off negative emotions.

DEATH STAR
An enormous Imperial battle station, which has enough firepower to destroy an entire planet.

DROID
A robot. Droids come in many shapes and sizes and serve a variety of duties.

EMPIRE
A tyrannical power that rules the galaxy under the leadership of Emperor Palpatine, a Sith Lord.

EMPEROR
Ruler of the Empire.

FORCE
The energy that flows through all living things. It can be used for good or evil.

FORCE-ENHANCED CLONE
A Force-powered clone created by Separatist leader and Sith apprentice Count Dooku.

FORCE LEAP
A huge jump made by someone using the Force to enhance their natural ability.

FORCE LIGHTNING
Deadly rays of blue energy used as a weapon.

FORCE PUSH
A blast of energy that a Force-user can create to knock over an opponent.

HOLOCRON
An ancient device that contains large amounts of data. It is activated through use of the Force.

JEDI
A member of the Jedi Order who studies the light side of the Force.

JEDI COUNCIL
Twelve senior Jedi who meet to make important decisions.

JEDI KNIGHT
A full member of the Jedi Order who has completed all of their training.

JEDI GRAND MASTER
The head of the Jedi Order and the greatest and wisest of the Jedi Masters.

JEDI MASTER
An experienced and high-ranking Jedi who has demonstrated great skill and dedication.

KYBER CRYSTAL
A very powerful crystal used in lightsabers. It greatly magnifies the powers of those who are sensitive to the Force.

LIGHTSABER
A sword-like weapon with a blade of pure energy that is used by Jedi and Sith.

LIGHT SIDE
The good side of the Force that brings peace and justice.

LIVING FORCE
The view that the Force is present in all living things. Those who live by this view rely on their instincts and live in the moment.

PADAWAN
A young Jedi apprentice who is in training to become a full-fledged Jedi Knight.

REBEL ALLIANCE
The organisation that resists and fights the Empire.

REPUBLIC
The democratic government that rules many planets in the galaxy.

SENATE
The government of the Republic. It is made up of senators from all over the galaxy.

SENATOR
A person who acts as a representative for their planet in the Senate.

SEPARATISTS
An alliance of those who are opposed to the Republic.

SITH
An ancient sect of Force-sensitives who seek to use the dark side of the Force to gain power.

YOUNGLING
A Force-sensitive child who joins the Jedi Order to be trained in the Jedi arts.

Senior Editor	**Hannah Dolan**
Editor	**Jo Casey**
Designer	**Rhys Thomas**
Additional Designers	**Jenny Edwards, Stefan Georgiou, Sam Richiardi, Anne Sharples**
Senior Pre-Production Producer	**Marc Staples**
Senior Producer	**Lloyd Robertson**
Managing Editor	**Paula Regan**
Design Manager	**Guy Harvey**
Art Director	**Lisa Lanzarini**
Publisher	**Julie Ferris**
Publishing Director	**Simon Beecroft**

Dorling Kindersley would like to thank Randi Sørensen, Paul Hansford, and Martin Leighton Lindhardt at the LEGO Group, and Jennifer Heddle and Ashley Leonard at Lucasfilm. Thanks also to Beth Davies, Shari Last, Julia March, Helen Murray, and Rosie Peet for editorial assistance.

First American Edition, 2016
Published in the United States by DK Publishing
345 Hudson Street, New York, New York 10014

Page design copyright ©2016 Dorling Kindersley Limited
DK, a division of Penguin Random House LLC
16 17 18 19 20 10 9 8 7 6 5 4 3 2 1
001–259630–May/16

A catalog record for this book is available from the Library of Congress.

ISBN 978-1-4654-5165-1

DK books are available at special discounts when purchased in bulk for sales promotions, premiums, fund-raising, or educational use. For details, contact: DK Publishing Special Markets, 345 Hudson Street, New York, New York 10014
SpecialSales@dk.com

Printed and bound in China

A WORLD OF IDEAS:
SEE ALL THERE IS TO KNOW

www.LEGO.com/starwars
www.starwars.com
www.dk.com